# THE

## CHRONICLES

SUSAN G. DEVAN

ISBN: 1466301287

ISBN 13: 9781466301283

*To Richard:*
*spouse, best friend and inspiration*

*Special thanks to Deb DiSandro of Slightly Off*
*and*
*Dianne Morr of Morr Creative Writing Services*

# ACKNOWLEDGMENTS

*The family and many friends of Emma Frick, known to everyone in Rock Bottom as Granny, have asked me to gather together the remembrances and anecdotes about this remarkable woman. In my capacity as editor of the Rock Bottom Rambler, I have had occasion to report many of Granny's adventures, misadventures and accomplishments. The best way to portray her life is to let those who share it relate their stories. I am indebted to Granny Frick's children: Radcliffe Frick and his wife Charlene, Emory and Duke Frick, and Irma Jean Tydings; her grandson Caltech Beck and his wife Laurie; Deputy Sheriff Billy Buster; TallMart Regional Manager Moore Byers; Rock Bottom Councilman Wheeler Diehl; Beehive Beauty Salon operator JoEllen Dyer; local sage Shadrach 'Crazy' Egan; On the Carpet TV talk show host Wynn Frey; wedding coordinator Sunny Hart; art teacher Viola Haze; Mavis Oxford, President of Tweeters, Cornrow County's Bird Watching Society; and I have added my own recollections. I also thank Emma Frick for writing two chapters that could only be told by her. Since Granny is still active in this community, I expect to have many more stories to relate someday.*

*Hunter Tydings, Editor*
*Rock Bottom Rambler, winner of county and statewide awards*
*for excellence in journalism.*

# CONTENTS

# 1

## GRANNY'S CRUSADE

*by*

*Radcliffe Frick*

Our town will never be the same without the Fruit Tarts and most everybody is blaming me for telling Maw about them dancing gals. My Maw, known as Granny Frick to folks in Rock Bottom, can be someone to reckon with when she gets something stuck in her craw, and she won't give up until she makes a situation right. The boys ain't happy about the Fruit Tarts closing down, and being the provider of liquid refreshment for the club, I ain't happy about the loss of business.

The trouble started when my brother Emory and me was smoking on the stoop, talking about the pretty gals at the club, and how they danced without no clothes on. We recollected how one

Amateur Night a customer with a little too much hooch under his belt got on stage, danced around and started peeling off his tee shirt. When Ernie run him off the stage he had collected two dollars from other customers! We had a big laugh over that. As luck would have it, Maw overheard us through the open window. For a woman over 50, Maw has hearing sharper than a coyote's. Growing up, we never caught on that she saw and heard everything we did. Well, when she caught the gist of what we was talking about, all hell broke loose!

"Radcliffe! Emory! Get your sorry selves in here! How dare you set right out there in public disgracing the name of Frick!"

That wasn't exactly right – I mean the part about being in public. Maw's house is set a good half mile from the nearest neighbor, and another two miles after that to the paved road.

"Get in here this minute, you worthless buzzards! You're going to tell me about this sinful place, and who runs it!" Maw was hanging out of the window and trying to whack us with a fly swatter. Her little gray eyes were squinched up and looking like steel, and her lips disappeared into a tight line. When Maw is in a fighting mood, there ain't no arguing the fine points. We couldn't object to being called worthless buzzards; Maw had real high hopes that some of her kids would make their mark in the world. Some would have called her snooty, but she named each of her boys after colleges. My brothers Emory and Duke could live with their names OK because they passed as solid country boys' names, but I always resented my real name, Radcliffe. When I found out that Radcliffe had been a girls' college I started calling myself just Cliff. My only sister, Irma Jean, narrowly escaped being named Marymount when Maw thought over the implications of carrying a name like that. Guess Irma Jean wanted to continue the family tradition, because she named her son Caltech; naturally we call him Cal most of the time. In spite of Maw's plans, none of us kids graduated from college. Every time one of us tries to better ourselves, the effort backfires and we get in deeper.

Anyways, soon as we slunk inside Maw lit into Emory and me about the Fruit Tarts. Maw's a real persistent cuss and you don't hold back on her, so we told her everything.

Emory, like the brother he is, froze up, hung his greasy head and blamed me for everything. At least he could have blamed our brother Duke, as I had been planning to do. Duke is due to be released by Sheriff Purgitt in a couple more days, and it would've been our word against his.

It's hard to believe Maw really didn't know about the club and dancing gals! Every man in town – and most school boys – knows what goes on at night in the back room of Ernie's Garden Supplies. There ain't no harm in it, near as I can tell. The boys get to relax, smoke, hoot at the ladies, and down some quality home brew supplied by yours truly. This has brought me real cash from time to time, and I like to think I'm bettering myself so Maw will be proud. Some of the gals do a little extra business on the side, but nothing like that ever happens on the premises at Ernie's.

I tried to stand up for what was right: "Now, Maw, it ain't no big deal. Growed men has a right to entertainment without their wives butting in. The business has been in town for at least ten years. Ernie has always run it, and every fella in town goes there." I just wished my voice hadn't sounded so quavery, like I was in grade school again and getting busted for drinking in the boys' room.

Maw was moving closer, like she was coming in for the kill. You'd think a man could stand up to a wiry old gal who only came up to his shoulder, but Maw was scary on a good day, and when she was mad, she could make you turn to jelly. I didn't want to back up, but did it anyways.

Emory was sniffling and scratching his armpit.

I tried again: " I just provide the drinks for the customers, and that's all…"

Maw poked a bony finger in my chest. "Not <u>every</u> man in town goes to that den of iniquity! Your Paw was a clean-living Christian gentleman who would've never been caught dead in a place like that. You boys ought to be ashamed to be seen there, and you, Radcliffe…"

"Cliff," I corrected her.

"…Radcliffe, are digging yourself a place in Hell by profiting off those sinful men; and what's more, you're corrupting Emory, here, who don't know what's up except what you teach him."

Emory came to life and tried to have his say. "Maw, it weren't Cliff took me there first, it were…" With this, I thumped Emory in the ribs with my elbow and shushed him. He was about to open up a whole new argument that we sure didn't want to be in. Better to take the hits ourselves. Lucky for us, Maw was fixing to take action and didn't hear anything.

"The Town Council and Sheriff Purgitt will hear about this, and those hussies will be driven out of town in less than a month. You have my word on that! Better find another outlet for your liquor, Radcliffe."

"But, Maw, Sheriff Purgitt is one of…" Emory don't have the sense he was born with. I had to punch him really hard this time.

I whined, sounding like an eight-year-old, "Aw, Maw, don't do this," but she wasn't listening.

"Emory, take the car parts off the passenger seat and drive me to town."

Emory was all mealy-mouthed, "OK, Maw." I grabbed him by the arm, and gave him a warning look. He knew what I meant.

Soon as they drove off, leaving dust and chicken feathers flying, I hightailed it in my own truck to Ernie's to give the Fruit Tarts a warning that Granny Frick was on the warpath and they better lie low for a while. The shop had already closed for the day, but tonight's show would have to be cancelled. Ernie Beck and I have always worked well together, him being family, sort of. He used to be married to Irma Jean, and my nephew Caltech is their son. I don't know exactly why they broke up, but I suspect the Fruit Tarts had something to do with that. Ernie does a real good job with the stage shows and lighting. I helped Ernie to decorate the place real classy, just like the Bubba Club over in Panhandle County, with old sheets stapled to the ceiling so that the colored lights shined on them. Sometimes when the air conditioning wasn't working it got stuffy in there and we had to open some windows. It gave a neat effect, the breeze blowing the sheets so they looked like waves, clouds or fire, depending on whether the blue, purple or red lights was on.

Emory gets music tapes, and I supply the liquid refreshment. Sheriff Jimmy Purgitt watches our backs in exchange for a few considerations. Lucky for me and Ernie, the Garden Supplies store was in a different direction from the Sheriff's office where Emory was taking Maw. This gave us a little time to hustle the ladies outside and into the trailers on the back lot. They grabbed everything they could carry, feathers and shiny little things falling on the floor as they ran through the shop and the potting shed. I helped Cherry carry stuff because she was a little bitty thing. I kind of liked Cherry anyways, because she always danced in red feathers and dyed her hair a real natural shade of bright red; I always got flustered when she danced.

Emory, being dumber than me, and not too picky about the women he flirted with, was partial to Peaches, who looked pretty enough but was getting a little old for the stage. Ernie always had to dim the lights some when Peaches danced, and I gave the boys extra hooch to keep their attention fuzzy. The other two Fruit Tarts were Honeydew and Berry. Honeydew was a hefty lady, and she could really shake her assets, as she called them. One evening a bug, the biggest beetle I ever saw, flew into the room and buzzed past my head right onto Honeydew's chest. You never heard such caterwauling! It took everybody ten minutes to catch that bug and calm her down. After that, Honeydew always danced with a feather boa, flinging it around her head and body so that we couldn't tell if she was dancing exotic or just swatting at flies.

Berry was a tall curvy black gal who used to go by Blackberry; Ernie thought that sounded too obvious, so she shortened her name to Berry. Altogether they was a sight to behold when they did their act in Ernie's back room. A man could unwind and forget his hard day when they shimmied.

We got the girls moved out, and tried to persuade them to lie low. Cherry wasn't too pleased with being uprooted, and said she was staying around to face the music when Maw and Sheriff Purgitt arrived. This sounded like the craziest thing I'd ever heard, and I told her so. Good-looking though she is, Cherry has a good heart and a lot of courage.

"Cliff, honey, it ain't right for your Maw to push you around like this; it's about time someone stood up to her, and I'm the one to do it. You're always miserable 'cause that woman has got you scooting with your tail between your legs."

"Cherry, you're a real sweetheart, but you don't know Maw. She can do things to a person just by narrowing her eyes at them. Old Crazy Egan up Turkey Hill swears she has the Evil Eye!"

"Cliff, you're silly and worrying about nothing. I will have a quiet private talk with Granny Frick, and - I promise - everything will die down. Cross my heart." With that she drew an X on her big soft chest and that so distracted me that I forgot how nervous I had been.

Just as we moved the last pile of the girls' stuff into their trailers behind the potting shed, Sheriff Purgitt's car came skidding into the lot. You could tell he was in a worried mood as he trotted into Ernie's. He did nod in my direction, "Hey, Cliff. Your mama's coming close on my heels, so I want to do some smoothing over before she gets here."

"I understand, Sheriff. She can be stubborn when she gets something on her mind, and the Fruit Tarts has her breathing fire."

A couple of the dancers came running when they seen the Sheriff's car pull up. They was out of breath, jiggling and bouncing. I loved it.

"Hey, Jimmy! Ain't seen you in a couple weeks. How you been? You gonna stay for the show?"

"Okay, Honeydew, Berry, I do miss you lovely things, but you got to listen up. Stay out of sight while Miz Frick is here, do you understand? If she gets wind of our, uh, friendship it'll be harder for me to keep you out of trouble. I see Cliff and Ernie have cleaned up the place." There was a trail of sequins and feathers that led straight to the back lot. If we had any luck, maybe Maw left her glasses at home.

All pouty, Berry and Honeydew hugged Jimmy Purgitt and stepped back out of sight just as Emory's rusty pickup bounced into the parking lot. Before Emory even turned off the engine, Maw popped out, her eyes smoking with righteous anger.

"Arrest them, Sheriff! These criminals has got to be put out of business for good. This town is no place for bawdy women and drunken lechers! You, Ernie, you slippery snake! You not only ruined Irma Jean's life, you've led my two boys down the road to sin and degradation."

"Three boys, Maw...," mumbled Emory. He never was very bright. Stubbornly, he began, "There's Duke, too..." but another thump hit its target and he hushed up.

Ernie threw up his hands, shook his head, and vanished into the back room.

Sheriff Purgitt hitched up his britches and cleared his throat. You could tell he was getting ready to pull rank on Maw while smoothing her ruffled feathers at the same time. "Now, Miz Frick, it ain't that easy. You can see there ain't no proof that anything unlawful has been taking place here. It's your word against Ernie's, and you heard it third-hand." His voice got soft and persuasive, "Besides, Miz Frick, your boys is involved and I'd have to arrest them, too. A lady with your fine reputation wouldn't want to be caught up in a public dispute that could have no good end, but would make headlines in the Rock Bottom Rambler."

This did nothing but set Maw off, and I was afraid she'd do something that would get her arrested for assaulting an officer of the law. She had a vicious grip on her big old heavy purse, and looked ready to swing it at him. Lucky for the Sheriff, Maw left Ol' Betsy the shotgun at home! Thank goodness she had also left her glasses home because she was stepping on sequins and feathers.

Suddenly, in the midst of this argument stepped a vision in red. I almost didn't recognize Cherry. She was wearing red, like always, but her outfit was a skirt and a loose-fitting sweater and her face was scrubbed clean. All the colorful makeup and sparkles was gone, and she looked like any nice lady you'd run into at TallMart. I tell you what, she looked just as pretty as ever, and I was seeing her in a new light.

Cherry's sweet voice piped up over the ruckus, "Miz Frick, you need to calm down. Come with me and we girls will talk, quiet-like."

Her boldness set Maw back on her heels. "Who the heck are you, young lady?"

I started to blurt out, "Maw, this here's Cher...," but Cherry interrupted me and looked straight into Maw's furious eyes without blinking.

"My name is Charlene, and you and I need to have a heart-to-heart, Miz Frick. Come on." With that, Cherry - or Charlene - took Maw's hand and led her into the potting shed, real gentle-like. They sat on a bench and started gabbing like they was old girl friends. The rest of us stood there flabbergasted.

Ernie said, "Who needs a drink?" Emory and Sheriff Purgitt bolted for the back room with Ernie, but I snuck under a bush near the open window of the shed. What I heard amazed me, not because I didn't already know the story, but because Cherry - Charlene, bless her heart - had the nerve to face Maw and shed some light on the truth.

"Miz Frick," she began, "you and I have had the pleasure of knowing the same sweet man."

Maw misunderstood what Charlene was getting at. "Hmmph! If you mean Radcliffe, I wouldn't use 'sweet' to describe him; well-meaning, maybe, but misguided." Then her voice got stormy again, "And if you're talking about that slimy Ernie Beck, ask my daughter Irma Jean just how 'sweet' he was when they was married!"

"No, Ma'am, I'm talking about Abner. Abner Frick."

Maw must've been struck dumb; she didn't say anything, but I could hear some sounds like shaky breathing and little sobs. I quietly stood up inside the bush, just so's I could see what was going on inside. Poor old Maw looked like she was all crumpled up, like a piece of paper that's been thrown away. Her eyes was all dull and sort of dead, not flashing like when she jumped out of Emory's truck. Truth sometimes really hurts. I felt sorry for Maw, but impressed with Cherry's courage. It takes some spunk to face down Maw, especially if you're the bringer of bad news. She had the good sense not to tell Maw that us boys used to come to Ernie's with Paw; he's the one that first brought us.

Charlene said, "Miz Frick, you got to listen to me. The truth is that your husband, Abner, was a regular customer at Ernie's." Here Maw whimpered and took out her hankie to wipe her nose. "Watching the Fruit Tarts shake their - I mean dance - helped him and the other guys relax and let off steam. Nothing else happened between me and Abner, or between him and any of the other girls, Miz Frick. You have my word on that. Ask Ernie. Ask the Fruit Tarts."

Maw finally pulled herself together and said, "Well, Miss - Charlene, is it? - All of us has secrets in our past," here she paused and her voice sounded lower and choked up, so I had to lean in closer to hear what she said, "even those of us you'd least suspect. Abner was a good man and a good husband. I never asked him about what he did with the boys, so he never told me. I thought one thing when he was doing another. What's done is done, but that don't change what's going on here and now. What's right is right, and I'm still going to see that Sheriff Purgitt shuts down this club." Some of her pepper was coming back. So was Cherry's.

"Oh, Miz Frick, you don't wanna do that. Jimmy Purgitt is one of our regulars, and so are your sons, even Duke when he gets out from time to time." Cherry's cheery voice began to sound a little bit colder and harder. "Just think how all the folks in town will read in the Rock Bottom Rambler about your family, Abner and the boys, being involved in a sexy scandal. Everybody at the church who knew Abner will be shocked; the old gals at your bingo games will find out; your grandson Cal and his fiancée will be embarrassed. You can see how it will be."

Maw looked hard at Cherry and her eyes narrowed, but she smiled a tight little smile. "Well, Missy, I got to hand it to you. I've met my match, and I got to admire somebody who stands up to me. Not many people do, not even my own spineless sons."

Now, that wasn't nice, but I was too caught up in the whole conversation to care about one offhand remark. Us boys is used to lots of them.

Maw went on, "You're right about the scandal and the mark on my Abner's reputation, Charlene; but all of us who has lived any length of time has had to weather many a storm. You have no idea! You think I haven't got used to people's wagging tongues? Remember, Duke and Radcliffe are my sons – enough said. I hoped to spare Radcliffe any sorrow where you are concerned, but

I can see by the way you look at each other that the two of you care for each other."

Now, that was a surprise to me, but Maw was right! I nearly lost my footing, and grabbed ahold of a thorny bush. Good thing Maw and Charlene was too caught up in their chat to notice my yelp.

"If you ever hurt Radcliffe, you'll have me to reckon with, and you ain't seen nothing yet. I'll agree not to press charges if you agree to two things."

Cherry was sweet as could be, "Whatever you say, Miz Frick. I do care for Cliff, and wouldn't ever do nothing to hurt him."

Maw said, "First, don't you ever tell anybody in Rock Bottom that Abner came here; second, break up the Fruit Tarts and don't ever dance in Ernie's Garden Supplies again."

Looking almost innocent, Cherry grinned and hugged Maw, who nearly fell off the bench. "Thank you, Miz Frick. You'll never hear of the Fruit Tarts any more."

True to her word, Maw asked the Sheriff to back off from arresting the gals, and he was happy to be let off the hook. Charlene never again went by the name Cherry, and none of the dancing girls ever told folks in town about Granny Frick's family secrets. The Fruit Tarts went out of business.

As the preacher says, though, the Lord will provide, and everything is working out just fine. Ernie's brother Jack Beck owns a hardware store on the other side of town, and it has a large shed out back just big enough to set up a small stage and a couple dozen folding chairs. The dancing girls made a comeback as the Budz. Cherry now dances as Rose; Honeydew's new name is Tiger Lily, Peaches is now known as Daisy; and Berry took the name Black-Eyed Susan. I still provide the liquid refreshment.

I began to look at Charlene with more than physical appreciation, if you know what I mean. She's a strong lady, and the only person I ever knew who could stand up to Maw. Maybe someday we can be a real couple and I can take her out dressed up fine in her red skirt and sweater. Maw won't be in a position to object.

Only one thing made me ponder: what "secrets of her past" was Maw referring to? They would come out all in good time.

# 2

# GRANNY AND THE GREMLINS

*by*

## *Caltech Beck*

I thought Granny Frick was just plain nuts when she said gremlins robbed her house, but now I know better. Some mean-minded old lady in town hinted that Granny had been hitting the bottle, and maybe that was the source of her "gremlins". That, of course, was just not true: if ever there was an upright Christian woman, Granny was it, and she wouldn't never of drunk any of Uncle Cliff's home brew – except maybe in a medical emergency like she has from time to time. No, the truth of what happened came to light, and it proved that Granny was no more nuts than any of the rest of the Frick clan. My Mama is Granny's daughter,

Irma Jean, who is hard-working and sensible, but my three uncles could be the Larry, Mo and Curly of Rock Bottom.

I'd best start from the beginning. Sheriff Purgitt got a call from Granny last Wednesday afternoon at three o'clock. Uncle Duke was with the sheriff at the time, on legal business of a sort. Granny was panicky, and babbling about her house being broken into by gremlins who shrieked at her and stole her valuables. A deputy rushed over to Granny's house, and our family members spread the word. We went there to give her our support even though we thought she was imagining things. Our clan may have problems sometimes, but when any of us is in trouble we are thick as thieves – maybe that's not a real good term to use.

Granny was pretty shaken up by the time we all arrived. She said, "I had just come down from the attic when I heard a noise at a front window. I walked into the room just as two hairy, mean-looking gremlins were climbing in." The deputy got a description from her, but it didn't make no sense. "They was short and butt-ugly," Granny said, "and noisy. I thought they was foreigners because they talked funny and were so uncivil. Them gremlins wore finer clothes than I can afford. They screamed and threatened me while they were tearing the place apart, and I was afraid they'd wreck my whole house. I scared them off with a blast from Ol' Betsy," and here she showed us the hole in the wall to prove it.

All that proved was that she fired the shotgun, it didn't prove there was gremlins in her house, except in her own mind. Her aim must've been off because she didn't hit the varmints, but Granny's always forgetting where she put her glasses and that could explain why she missed. We was all doubting her, and that was understandable. The house was a real mess, and some things was missing, but we figured Granny had Fee-Bayed some of her valuables and was shamed to tell us. The string of pearls Grandpappy had given her when they got married was gone, and so was his gold pocket watch that she took out of her drawer and cried over sometimes. The silver spoons was missing that her mama had bought in Chicago on her honeymoon. Selling her valuables on Fee-Bay would of given Granny the cash to take that bus trip last month to the outlet mall in River County, where she bought her new genuine snakeskin shoulder strap for Ol' Betsy. Personally, I didn't believe it made much sense that Granny would Fee-Bay things that meant so much to her, but what else could we think?

"Wait a minute, Maw," said Uncle Emory, "how come you're home today? Ain't Wednesday your hairdresser day? Don't you usually get your hair blued around this time?" He seemed jittery and worried, and that made me wonder.

"Used to, boy, but I had to switch days. Seems JoEllen had to give up Wednesdays so's to take her kid to baton twirling lessons. Now I go on Thursdays. Come to think of it, why ain't you at your job today?"

Here she squinted at Uncle Emory real close. "You get fired again?"

"No, Maw. Just started a job with a new fella – a buddy of mine – and looking to make some big money. You'll be proud of me real soon."

Her only reply to that was "Hmmph!"

The deputy promised to look into the case, but we felt that Granny had seen the last of her valuables no matter how they had disappeared. I had plans with my girl Laurie that evening and didn't want to disappoint her, but I didn't like to think of Granny all alone and frightened in that messy old house with them gremlins, or whatever they were, still on the loose. Uncle Cliff mumbled as how he had stuff to attend to. Uncle Emory was nervous as a rabbit and couldn't wait to go somewhere and meet up with his new business partner. Uncle Duke was still in custody. Mama had to do her shift at the plant, so that left me to console Granny.

"Say, Granny, you need to get out of this place and calm your nerves. How's about going to the Cornrow County Fair with me and Laurie this evening?"

"Why, Caltech, you are a sweet old thing, but I don't want to be a burden. You young folks go ahead. I got Ol' Betsy. We chased them gremlins away once, and we can do it again."

The thought of Granny shooting up her house over gremlins bothered me, so I insisted. "You got to come, Granny! How many years since you been to the County Fair? There are some great shows you'll enjoy, and them corn dogs you like so much. Some fella can guess your age and weight, and if he's wrong you get a prize. The boys has got their old cars on display; bet you'll find one you used to ride in when you were young! One show has ponies and parrots that do tricks. And guess who's singing tonight? Bucky Burke and the Bail-Jumpers! Change your mind?"

At mention of Bucky Burke, Granny's gray eyes lit up. "Caltech, you always could persuade me! All right, it might do me some good."

That settled it. Laurie and me picked up Granny that evening and headed for the Cornrow County Fair. Granny loved the lights and the excitement. She ate three corn dogs and tried her skills at the shooting booth. Good thing she remembered her glasses, because she won an Elvis pillow. She loved most everything she saw that night, but turned up her nose at the prize-winning pies because hers were better.

"Come on, Caltech, you and me've got to go on the Tilt-a-Whirl; that was always my favorite ride, and your Grandpappy would never go on it with me."

I grabbed my stomach and made a sour face. "Granny, I can't go on it, either. I always get sick when I ride that thing, and them corn dogs didn't set too well, anyways."

"That's all right, Granny," said Laurie, bless her heart, "I love the Tilt-a-Whirl, so I'll ride it with you." Saved by Laurie again! The two of them rode the thing twice in a row, laughing and rocking the seat back and forth to make it spin wildly when the big curve came up. It almost made me queasy just to watch. When they got off, Granny bought two more corn dogs because, she said, "All that exercise made me hungry."

Granny flirted with Bucky Burke while he was singing good old cheating-heart country songs. "Ain't he handsome?" she asked, with dreamy looks at Bucky, who played it up and flirted right back at her. Bucky Burke had a bad reputation as a conniving weasel who lied to ladies of all ages and cheated on his wife. I was beginning to think I might have a problem on my hands, and told Laurie about it. The bum even tried to flirt with Laurie, but she gave him a look that put him in his place. As soon as the Bail-Jumpers' last song was done, we turned Granny's attention to the animal acts in a dusty ring near the livestock pens.

Granny couldn't keep her eyes off the animals doing their tricks. The night before, Laurie and me had seen this fella's ponies that could count and stand on their hind legs while parrots sat on their heads, but Wednesday night he had other animals doing tricks for the crowd. A pack of silly fluffy dogs with funny hats did all sorts of acrobatics, jumping through hoops and walking across boards on their hind legs. Granny laughed and clapped like a little kid. The fair was definitely the best medicine for her that night!

Suddenly, Granny dropped her Elvis pillow and yelled out. She staggered back against me, and nearly fell down. Eyes wide open in fright, she pointed with shaky fingers at the next act coming into the ring: two chimpanzees were galloping around and doing somersaults and other tricks. They were dressed in little suits and ties, and they walked around on two legs just like people.

"It's them!" Granny shrieked. "It's the gremlins! Help! Somebody get the sheriff! They stole my things!" Granny's screaming made everyone, including the monkeys, stop and look at her. The chimpanzees, hearing Granny's voice, must have recognized her as the one who took a pot shot at them in her house. They started screaming, too, and raced around in the ring. The trainer looked scared and confused, and tried to catch the chimpanzees, but they was so rattled that one of them bit him. Poor Elvis was getting stomped on and ripped when the chimps attacked the pillow with their teeth. They whapped a few people with it, upset the corn dog cart, opened the gate to the performing ring, and let the animals free. Sheriff Purgitt and the Deputy, never far away whenever the fair is on, showed up just in time.

Out of nowhere, who should appear but Uncle Emory! He came from the animal trainer's tent and tried to catch the monkeys. Dogs was barking, parrots squawking and ponies neighing somewhere, and the crowd was turning into a mob. Handing Granny over to Laurie, I jumped into the ring and tackled the trainer, pinning him down and sitting on him. He had to be in on the robbery with Uncle Emory, who didn't have enough smarts to train monkeys to do nothing.

Uncle Emory, realizing by now that the cat – or the monkey - was out of the bag, run up to Granny and tried to explain how he didn't know the chimpanzees were going to rob her house, and he was real sorry and it wouldn't happen again. Granny wasn't about to let him off the hook so easy, and if the Sheriff hadn't stopped her I think she'd have attacked Uncle Emory.

"I ain't that dumb, you little buzzard! You're due for your come-uppance, and you deserve every minute you spend with your brother Duke! Who else but family knew about my silver spoons and pearls and bottle cap collection ?"

Uncle Emory got real depressed and just sat down in the dirt with his head on his hands. The Sheriff arrested both him and the animal trainer. In a trunk in the trainer's tent the Deputy Sheriff found Granny's valuables, as well as stuff from other folks who must of been robbed last week, too. Granny hit her son Emory with the dirty, trampled Elvis pillow as he was being led away in cuffs, and, Christian woman though she is, she let loose with a few words that we didn't know she knew.

Sheriff Purgitt called me aside when the thieves had been loaded up and driven off. "Cal, I'm real impressed with your quick thinking and fast action tonight. My Department can use a young fella like you on the force; you interested?"

"Now that you mention it, Sheriff, I've been thinking about that lately. I may even go to one of them colleges some day and study law enforcement!" Laurie was impressed, too, and that's another story.

Sheriff Purgitt looks to be a shoe-in for re-election. JoEllen shared some of the credit because if she hadn't changed Granny's hairdressing day she wouldn't of been home when the gremlins broke in. Granny was the talk of the town, and got her picture on the front page of the local newspaper, the Rock Bottom Rambler. The headline read: Local Granny Clobbers Chimp Robbers, and the caption under her picture said, "Emma Frick, intrepid crime stopper."

Our family learned two good lessons from all this: when Granny Frick sees gremlins, better believe she saw something, and if you have to be on the wrong side of the law, be sure not to involve Granny in it!

Lucky for Uncle Emory, the judge went easy on him. He said something about "congenital intellectual disability" and "diminished capacity", whatever that is, and blamed most of the crime on the business partner, who had a record a mile long in Panhandle and River Counties, and in several counties in the next state. The judge said that "a simpleton like Emory was susceptible to being influenced by a seasoned crook". Uncle Emory said he suspected he should feel insulted, but didn't quite know why.

# 3

# GRANNY TAKES A JOB

*by*

*Moore Byers*

Once upon a time in Panhandle County, the center of the universe was the local TallMart, my store. I am Moore Byers; I have managed this store for ten years, and pride myself on our excellent customer service, spotless rest rooms, and financial stability. I run my TallMart efficiently, with almost military precision. We are the envy of retail businesses in the Tri-County region, receiving frequent awards from TallMart management and from local Chambers of Commerce.

The peace was shattered one day when Emma Frick, known down the road in Cornrow County as "Granny", applied to work in TallMart as a greeter. There were only three applicants for the job that week. One had a police record for serial shoplifting, and another seemed to be in the early stages of dementia, so that left Miz Frick. She was a sharp old gal and looked like she could take on anybody, so we hired her on the spot, and trained her that week. The first hint that Miz Frick would be a challenge was her disregard for job descriptions, employees' dress codes, and rules about acceptable behavior on the job. Training her in proper procedures was a battle.

"You mean, I have to stand at the door and be nice to everybody? What if they're up to mischief?" Granny disagreed with store policy of not apprehending shoplifters ourselves, but letting the police conduct their own investigations and arrests.

"Ain't nobody going to tell me what to wear," she added.

"But, Miz Frick," I explained, "all employees have to dress according to our code; it makes them easily identifiable to shoppers, and just keeps everything – you know – *orderly*." "I can't afford to go out and buy green pants and yellow shirts just on your account. I can work just as well in my regular clothes; if calico skirts gets folks riled up, then they'll just have to look the other way."

With a sigh of resignation, I agreed to make an exception in Granny's case. I suspected it wouldn't be long before she became the most identifiable employee in the store.

"You will receive the 10% employee discount at TallMart, Miz Frick," I told her, expecting her to be as excited as other senior citizen greeters when they learn about their perqs.

"Don't worry about that, sonny," said Granny, "I don't shop here; I go to the BullsEye five miles east of here. They give lots of sales and two-fers, like 'Buy two chainsaws for the price of one'." I could tell that working with Granny was going to be an adventure, but what could we do? With our big sale coming up we needed another greeter, and I was touched by Miz Frick's desire to help out her family members who needed cash for various enterprises.

The moment of truth arrived: Granny Frick's first day on the job. It was a balmy spring morning, guaranteed to bring out shoppers in the droves. We had marked up everything in the store in preparation for the big sale. I lined up our troops and gave them a pep talk, reminding them of TallMart's renowned Public Information Satisfaction Survey (P.I.S.S.). P.I.S.S. holds our employees to a standard of excellence in the way they treat customers and answer their questions. The employees who receive the most commendations from the public survey each month receive a gift certificate, and are eligible to compete for the coveted prize in December, the Customer Relations Annual Prize (C.R.A.P.).

The hubbub of shoppers was music to my ears: voices chattering, plastic bags crinkling, babies crying, country music on the speaker system, cash registers clicking, Granny Frick yapping...? What was going on? I hurried to the main door, where people were backed up and there was a commotion. Miz Frick stood in the midst of a knot of shoppers. Her voice rang out insistently.

"Oh, no, you don't, buster! I'm in charge here, and I say you're not going into this here store!"

"Out of the way, you crazy old woman! You have no right to keep us out!"

I tried to step in. "Calm down everybody, what's the problem?"

"This woman says we can't go into the store! She can't do that!"

I took one look at the family, and secretly had to agree with Granny that they were a scurvy-looking bunch, but if I turned away every unkempt TallMart shopper we'd have an empty store. Taking Granny aside, I said, "Miz Frick, I can see your point about these customers, but we would get into a lot of legal trouble if we refuse to let them come in. What is your objection to these folks?"

Granny, planted at her post like a bulldog, replied, "I know all about them buzzards, Mr. Breyers..."

"Byers", I interjected, "the name is Byers."

"...they used to hang around with my son Duke, and they're thieves and pickpockets. I wouldn't let him bring them into my house, and I won't let them into my TallMart!"

I thanked Granny for her concern and made her promise to admit the family if I kept extra close watch on them. She grudgingly agreed, and the motley crew entered the store carrying oversized bags and wearing unseasonably bulky coats and jackets. Before the morning was over, security spotted several members of the group stuffing merchandise into bags and clothing. We notified the local law enforcement authorities, who were waiting for them as they left the store.

I wanted to thank Miz Frick for her heads-up on the shoplifting gang, and caught up with her in the produce section; she was enjoying a snack at our expense from the bakery and fresh fruit sections. "Oh, no, Miz Frick!" I exclaimed. "You cannot help yourself to food here; you must pay for it!"

"I ain't been paid for my day's work yet, sonny. How do you expect me to have the strength to keep crooks out of your store if I'm faint with hunger? My son Emory won't be here to pick me up for another hour; he has to see his parole officer first."

"Granny, I appreciate your sharp eye on the job today, so just this once I will personally pay for your food. Hereafter, though, please brown bag your snack; it will not look good if other employees see you snitching food." I had to admit that Granny had saved us many dollars that day. We should have hired her as Head of Security. The police recovered merchandise worth many hundreds of dollars from the possession of the shoplifters. It did worry me that Granny's sons were too familiar with the process, and I decided to keep an eye on them if they came into TallMart.

The next morning went more smoothly. Granny was dressed up in smiles and nods for all the customers, and they seemed unusually pleased to see the greeter. Closer inspection at the door revealed Granny was handing out cookies to shoppers as they entered TallMart.

"Miz Frick." I said sternly, "where did you get those cookies?" I thought she had raided the bakery department again.

"Hold your horses, sonny," she said, "I baked these myself for all my friends."

"Should I ask what you are up to? This is unheard of."

"It's plain that the best-liked employee will get the P.I.S.S. and C.R.A.P. awards, and I intend to be that person. What better way to win folks over than with the best cookies in the Tri-County region?"

"Granny, I confess I admire your resourcefulness, but I have to discourage you from bringing food from outside into this store. If anything happened, TallMart would get sued, and there would go my job, your job, C.R.A.P., and everything else…"

That evening when we opened the box with commendation slips filled out by satisfied customers, over 90% of them were votes for Granny Frick, "that nice blue-haired lady in the pretty bright colored skirt."

For a while it seemed that things had settled down at the main door, with Granny finally doing the job she had been hired to do, and nothing more. One morning, as I made the rounds of the departments, I noticed something slightly off in the displays. The merchandise was arranged according to no pattern I recognized. At an end cap I discovered why: there was Emma Frick, busily shifting items around.

"So, Miz Frick, hard at work, are we?" I had a hard time disguising the irritation I was feeling.

"Don't know about you, Mr. Breyers, but I sure am. These shelves is a mess, and I'm straightening them out for you. Like what you see?"

"I don't know, what am I looking at?"

"To me, it made more sense to put bedroom things together that were the same color. That way, if someone sees a new shade of blue sheets, naturally they'll decide to buy new blankets, comforters, lamps and curtains, and that'll dress up their bedroom real nice."

"Naturally," I replied.

"And that's not all. There was some mirrors with lights all round; you know, the kind that ladies use to put on their makeup. So, I decided to put some lipstick and mascara and other stuff like that with the mirrors, to kind of inspire them what they could do to theirselves if they had one of them contraptions."

Taking a deep breath to calm myself, I said, "Granny, you mean well, but you are a greeter, and that's all. These displays will all be put back the way they belong, but from the extent of the rearranging you have done, it will take us more than one evening and some extra manpower. This is your last warning to do things the way I want them done, or I will be forced to dismiss you. Clear? And the name is Byers."

Immediately, I hated myself. Granny's face looked crestfallen, and her gray eyes watered up. I felt as if I had kicked a puppy, so I quickly added, "You are the best greeter I've ever had, so I'm counting on you at the main door."

With that, she nodded and returned to her post.

The sales for the next couple of days showed a sharp increase in the linens department, especially in color-coordinated bedding, and sales of both vanity mirrors and assorted cosmetics jumped. P.I.S.S. feedback complimented our innovative marketing of merchandise, and specifically lauded the customer service given by the "little lady changing displays, who gave full credit to the store manager, since it was his idea".

Miz Frick's unorthodox methods aroused the jealousy of other employees, who could see their chances at the monthly P.I.S.S. award melting away. They reported her for turning away business by advising customers they could find the same items cheaper at the BullsEye (which, although true, is not something we spread around). They said she gave unsolicited advice on style and color to clothes buyers, and discouraged the purchase of store specials in favor of less expensive merchandise. The most serious report involved a woman who came into TallMart and headed for the jewelry department where Granny, naturally, was rearranging the counter.

"That there's a real pretty brooch," said Granny,

The young lady beamed and answered, "Isn't it lovely? My husband gave it to me for no reason at all! Isn't he the sweetest thing? He said it's got real diamond chips in it."

"And you've come to check it out, ain't you? Maybe even see how much it cost him?"

The woman was flustered because that was, indeed, why she was there.

Granny continued, "He was right, Missy, those are diamond chips; I remember him coming in last week and buying two of them pins. Said one was a birthday gift for his special gal. You're a lucky lady, ain't you? Maybe his Ma is the other gal."

The customer broke out in tears and raced out of the store; we thought surely we were going to be sued, but that was not the case.

She came back in and filled out a P.I.S.S. form thanking Granny for confirming what she had suspected all along about her husband's "other gal". Out of her award in the divorce settlement she donated a hefty sum to our program for coats for needy children.

It was hard to discipline Granny for these infractions, since sales in our branch were soaring. The customers she advised filled out commendation slips for her, putting her even farther out in front in the race for C.R.A.P. Granny consistently won the monthly P.I.S.S. awards – and donated the gift certificates to our poorer customers. In December the C.R.A.P., to no one's surprise, went to Granny, who said the $1,500 would be spent on her grandson's college education, and as her friends we'd all be invited to his graduation party. As a result of my TallMart's success, I was made Regional Manager of the Tri-County area, and will be happy to help Granny Frick and her family celebrate.

After the frenetic days of holiday shopping and returns, Granny approached me. "Mr. Byers, the time has come. My job here is done and I'm giving you my notice."

In a panic at first, I couldn't imagine our TallMart without the intrepid Emma Frick running the store. "Miz Frick!" I cried, "How can you leave us? We made such a good team."

"Sonny, you ain't going to be manager of this store; you're going to be taking care of the whole region. You don't need me for that. I earned the money I needed for my kids."

I couldn't believe I was going to miss her. Seeing my reluctance to say good-bye, Granny said, "Well, Mr. Regional Manager, for the same amount of money you paid me here, I'd be willing to work for you as a secret shopper – just to, you know, keep an eye on the store and the new manager, and report to you if things ain't right. Deal?"

Delighted, I replied, "Deal, Miz Frick."

"Good. Now I can save up for that genuine faux leather recliner I spotted at BullsEye last week!"

# GRANNY GETS ARRESTED

## by
## *Caltech Beck*

**W**hoever said Hell ain't got no fury like a woman must of seen my Granny get riled up at a Bingo game. I was there once when she got into an argument, and I almost took pity on the poor soul who started it. Naturally, the other gal made the first move. Granny being a Christian woman, she wouldn't never of started trouble.

Granny called me late one afternoon. "Caltech," she said, as sweet as candy, "your Mama's got the evening shift at the plant this week, and I had my heart set on Bingo. Can you pick me up at 6:15 so's we can make the Early Bird?"

In any small town the Volunteer Fire Department's weekly Bingo game is serious business, as everyone knows, but to Granny it was a mission.

"Aw, Granny, shoot! Me 'n' Laurie was going bowling tonight! How's about next week?"

Granny sounded disappointed. "The jackpot's up to $793 this week, Caltech. You and Laurie might win some money if you come. I'll pay for your cards and hot dogs, and you won't have to spend a dime."

The thought of not having to spend money was real good. Me and Laurie was saving up to get married, and Laurie didn't mind hanging out with Granny, who is a hoot. I didn't want to give in too easy, though.

"Well, I don't know. Gas is high, and the Fire Hall's the other side of town…"

"Boy, I'll buy gas for your truck! Just say you'll do it!" She was excited enough to agree to anything, so I pretended to give in and clapped myself on the back for getting free gas. Granny even said she'd split her winnings with Laurie and me fifty-fifty, for our wedding fund. Granny may be a bit feisty sometimes, but it's usually when she's been wronged, and she is always generous with folks. Also, she's never boring! She says she'll dance at our wedding, and that's a sight we can't wait to see!

Laurie took the new plans in stride like the sweet thing she is. "Cal, honey, I love Granny, and I'll play Bingo with her and go to the county fair with her, but there's one thing I'll never do."

"What's that, punkin?"

"I will never name our kids after colleges like your Granny done to your uncles and your Mama done to you! She's already hinting that she never got around to Baylor and Rice, and I think she expects us to take up where she left off."

I had to admit I was with Laurie one hundred percent on this.

"You know I wouldn't allow that, either, punkin. We can pick out everyday names like Dale or Rusty…"

"Or Tammy or Reba…"

As you can tell, we are a good match, and never argue about nothing.

Laurie stuffed herself into the little space behind the truck seats, and Granny climbed aboard. Her bag was jingling and clicking. Granny had brought her own equipment to the Bingo game like she always does: colored indelible markers for special paper Bingo cards, round metal buttons for regular cardboard ones, and magnetic clickers that put buttons on the cards one by one and pick them up after each game so that you don't even have to touch them. She had made her own Bingo bag and painted her name on it in bright colors: Emma Frick, Bingo Nut. She couldn't of been more ready if she was going to war.

When we walked into the hall, you could smell the excitement. Actually, what you could smell was smoke. Even though there was No Smoking signs posted, every old gal there had a cigarette pasted to her lips, and the air was thick and blue. None of the old fellas running the game would ever take their life in their hands by making one of them Bingo players get rid of a butt. Granny was no exception. Before we even got the cards she was digging around in her bag for her smokes. "Boy," she once told me, "the good Lord made tobacco so's we could smoke it. Who am I to refuse His gift? If it ain't killed me yet, I ain't worried about tomorrow." Hard to argue with that, so I don't try any more.

We wandered through the hall, trying to find a good table near the caller so Granny wouldn't have to walk far to claim her winnings. The real serious players was already set up, and Granny was itching to join them. She bought herself fifteen cards, and three each for me and Laurie. The folks at the tables each had at least that many, some more. Most of the players was women, but a few brave men showed up because they was dragged there by the ladies. People squinted at us through the smoke and glared, real mean-like. I knew what they was thinking: the jackpot was almost $800, and they didn't like extra folks showing up to be their competition, especially if we wasn't regulars. Some of them mumbled under their breath and puffed harder on their cigarettes. The hall was full of horsetail-black and blonde and fiery red and half-bald heads bobbing over their cards and turning to size us up. It was easy to spot Granny because her hair was blued – "oh-natural" she called it.

While Granny found a table and arranged her cards me and Laurie went for hot dogs and lemonade. When we got back, she was raring to go, all settled in and guarding her spot. Got to hand it to her, Granny could glare right back at those old gals, giving them as good as they gave. She wore a red sweater that night because she once heard red was a "power color", whatever that means, and if it was power they wanted to see, she'd oblige. Her red indelible marker matched her sweater.

The sound of shuffling and clicking began to get slower, sort of like popcorn that is almost done and is going to burn if you leave it in any longer. Then old man Mooney tested the microphone and turned on the lighted board that showed which numbers had been called. There were a few squeals, a few sighs and low comments, but mostly a deafening noise of dozens of old ladies coughing; guess they was clearing their lungs so they'd live long enough to win the jackpot.

Granny got out her lucky charm, a bobble head Ronald Reagan, and set him down on the table next to the ashtray where she could rub his head when the pressure was on.

Just as Mr. Mooney was ready to call the first regular game of the evening, a mean-looking old lady with a brown scrunchie hat grabbed the seat across the table from Granny.

Big mistake.

She dumped her stuff out in a pile and plopped her big self down, huffing and puffing, just in time to spread out her four Bingo cards and light a cigarette. Her bright lipstick spread across the wrinkles around her mouth, so when she blew smoke in Granny Frick's direction her lips puckered up into a pink spider web. Her rude behavior pissed Granny, who blew her own smelly smoke back across the table. Granny muttered some not-so-Christian insults under her breath and rearranged Ronald Reagan with a thump. Ol' Miz Brown Hat brought out her own lucky charm – a little ceramic skunk - and the two ladies glared at each other like cats facing off over a dead mouse.

I decided to be friendly, and make peace. "Hey! How y'all doing? Ready to win tonight?"

Granny thumped me in the side with her elbow and grunted.

The old lady across the table answered me, "You bet, sonny. And nobody better stand in my way." With that she gave another sour look at Granny.

The clatter of the Bingo cage turning got everyone's attention. Them little balls bounced around until one fell into the cup and Mooney called out the first number: "B-6!" Groans and whispers followed, and the sound of clicking as the holders of cards with B-6 on them put their metal disks on the spot. Laurie had B-6 on two of her cards, so we was off to a good start. As happens sometimes in Bingo, some lucky player got Bingo after only four calls: one number under B, I, G and O, and of course the Free Space under N. The number O-69 was hardly out of Mr. Mooney's mouth when the clicking started: dozens of old ladies gathering up their markers with their magnetic toys. There were lots of mean looks, grumbling, and lighting of fresh cigarettes.

Since that was only a regular game, most took their loss lightly. The real prize they had come to get was the $793 jackpot. It would be awarded to the winner of a special game that cost extra and was played on paper cards. We sat through lots of regular games, and Laurie won a couple of them. Granny won one special game, where we had to cover the squares in the four corners of the card, which is not as easy as it sounds. She squealed and knocked Ronald Reagan over in her excitement, and collected $65. The old lady across from us was disgusted and threw her used cards on the floor, marked with her bright pink ink; she had three of the four corners on one of them and wasn't happy to lose!

The evening went on and on, but it wasn't really boring. You kind of get into the thrill of winning and the disappointment of having only one more square to cover when somebody yells out "Bingo!" You get greedy to buy more and more of the special cards, and more and more impatient for the big moment when the jackpot game will be played. It was amazing to watch Granny minding all them cards at once, and she never missed a beat. It was almost like being on line at the plant, where you have to watch what you're doing every minute or you'll mess up.

Laurie and me did pretty good, though we didn't win $65 all at once like Granny did. At last, toward the end of the evening, the special cards for the jackpot game went on sale, and what a commotion! It seemed the more those folks had lost during the evening, the more they were going to try and make it up during the jackpot game, so they spent their last few dollars on the little paper cards that would make them big winners at last. Granny bought one each for me and Laurie, and fifteen for herself.

A dead silence fell on the hall. The players held on tight to their colored markers, and looked daggers at each other, like they was daring someone to rob them of their prize. The cage clacked and the first number was drawn: "I-18!"

There was the usual groans and whispers, and the thudding sound of markers all over the hall hitting I-18 on the cards of the luckier players. This was going to be a long game because the winner had to cover every one of the numbers on their card. So far so good. Granny had I-18 on five of her fifteen cards. Laurie and me didn't have it at all.

Granny was so tense that she forgot to smoke her cigarette, and the ash grew longer and longer until it fell onto the table. Her sharp gray eyes were fixed on the cards like her life depended on the outcome of the game.

Old Lady Brown Hat across the table from us was antsy; she was acting shifty and nervous, and kept watching Granny's cards almost as much as she watched her own six.

Granny was doing great this time, and one of her cards was almost filled up before most of us had got a decent start. Finally, she had only one empty number to cover when a commotion broke out. Miz Brown Hat started coughing up a storm, and while she was grabbing for her thermos and a tissue she scrambled the Bingo cards that she and Granny had been marking! Some was dropped on the floor, and she hurried and picked them up just as her coughing spell was stopping. Granny yelped like she had been shot, and dove under the table to fight over the spilled cards with the other woman.

Just then the last number was called, "G-52". Granny howled, "No!" and other things I won't repeat. She was desperate to find her almost-filled card, because she knew that G-52 was the only number she had left to cover. The other players caught on that someone was real close to winning that jackpot, and they joined in the ruckus.

Mr. Mooney wrung his hands and asked, "Was that a Bingo?"

Granny screamed again, "No! I mean, yes!" Try as she might, she couldn't find that card.

The woman across the table from us yelled, "Bingo!" The crowd was shocked at the quickness of the win, and the angry voices sounded like a roar.

Granny looked again at her cards, and squawked, "Hold it! That ain't her Bingo! She stole my card!"

"Did not!" snapped Brown Hat, "Count your cards. I still have only six."

"You switched one, you varmint!" screamed Granny. "Give it to me, or I'll call the cops!" With that, she waved Ronald Reagan in the old lady's face like she was going to hit her with him, but of course Granny wouldn't never do that. She grabbed for the card! They had a tug of war, and it got crumpled and torn.

"Look what you did, you ...," said the woman, and I'll not repeat the name she called Granny.

The two ladies was really brawling. Granny threw the old lady's hat on the floor and stomped on it, and the woman yanked Reagan's bobble head so hard that the spring was stretched and his neck was 10 inches long. Both of them was swinging their Bingo bags and whapping each other with them. Granny wouldn't listen to me or Laurie, and we didn't want to hold her down with force. Poor old Mr. Mooney was all confused, running back and forth and holding his head. He was not about to step in between two women having an argument, so he called Sheriff Jimmy Purgitt to come and do it for him.

When the Sheriff rushed in, he and the deputy each held onto one of the women and tried to calm them down, but they was having none of it.

"Arrest this woman, Sheriff!" yelled Brown Hat (without it she was more like Bald Head). "She's trying to cheat me out of my winnings!" It was easy for someone who didn't know Granny to think that the old lady was telling the truth.

Granny was filled with righteous wrath at being robbed, and was fighting hard for that $793. "I ain't the thief, Jimmy Purgitt! This woman stole my card deliberate, and you need to arrest her!"

Mooney timidly picked up the wrecked card and gave it to the officers as evidence. They instructed the crowd to remain in place until the matter was settled, then carted Granny and the other lady – identified by Mr. Mooney as regular Bingo player Miz Hanks - off to the station. Me and Laurie cleaned up the mess they left behind. I pocketed a couple of things to show the Sheriff once we got to the jail to get Granny out of her jam.

Sure enough, the scene at the station was as bad as it had been at the Fire Hall; the two old ladies was tossing insults at each other, and Granny was charging the other woman with stealing her winning card and robbing her of the prize money.

Uncle Duke was there in a nearby cell, having been picked up on one of the usual charges. "Howdy, Maw!" he said, real happy-like. "What you doing here?"

"Hush up, Duke" snapped Granny.

Then Laurie took Sheriff Purgitt aside and talked to him real quiet, saying we had proof that Granny had been robbed. He was ready to listen to her because he was her Mama's brother, and knew her to be a smart and respectful girl, whereas not all of his dealings with my clan had been too satisfying. Turning to his deputy, he said, "Watch these two for a few minutes, and whatever you do, don't let them go at each other again."

The poor deputy looked like he had just been sentenced to a firing squad, but he hitched up his britches and tried to stand taller.

"All right, Laurie, what's this proof you're talking about?"

"Take a look at the winning card, Uncle Jimmy. Cal, show the Sheriff what you brought with us."

I reached into my pocket and gave him the two markers that Granny and Miz Hanks had been using, and some of the special paper cards marked in red and pink.

Granny and Miz Hanks had gotten real quiet, and were leaning forward the better to hear what was being said in our corner of the room.

"You see? Granny Frick was using the red marker that matched her sweater," said Laurie, "and the other woman was using a bright pink one. The winning card is marked mostly in red; only the last number called, G-52, is covered with pink marker."

Granny yipped, "See there? Told you it was my card she stole!"

Miz Hanks was frowning and looking stubborn. "Don't mean nothing! She took my marker and used it."

I added, "If you look at the old gals' fingers, you'll see that Granny's are stained red because she was using a red marker all evening, and the other lady's are stained pink!"

Sheriff Purgitt was right impressed. "Good work, kids! Ain't no point in filing charges against either of these gals; it would cost the county more than the Bingo prize was worth. I'll escort the ladies back to the Fire Hall and tell Mr. Mooney who was the true winner tonight. I'll give Miz Hanks a good talking-to right there in front of the Bingo crowd, and that should set her straight. She'll probably not come near the place for a long time." Then he looked hard at Granny, "Of course, Miz Frick would do well to control herself in public. She does have an excitable nature!"

Laurie, coming to Granny's defense, said, "She had a right to be upset, Uncle Jimmy! There was over $700 at stake, and that mean old lady was cheating her out of it! Worst of all, Ronald Reagan was violated!" I couldn't of said it better. You can see why I'm so crazy about Laurie!

Granny was grinning from ear to ear. "Thanks to you two youngsters – and you, too, Jimmy Purgitt – I'm getting the jackpot money I won fair and square. That's enough for me."

Before we left, the Sheriff said to me, "I hope you're still considering the offer I made to you once; we could use a young fella like you on the force."

"It's been on my mind, sir," I answered, "and I plan to do that someday. I'm enrolled in South Hollow Institute of Technology, working toward a degree in Criminal Investigation. I'm getting plenty of practice just taking Granny around and trying to keep her out of trouble!"

Laurie and me said, "So long, Uncle Duke," to which he replied, "See you in two-three days!" He was entirely too happy for a man who had just been jailed, but we figured he had been sampling a little too much of Uncle Cliff's special brew. At least he and Granny wouldn't be sharing a cell this night.

We arranged to meet Granny and the Sheriff at the Fire Hall, where she could collect her $793 and let us take her home. Granny was splitting her winnings with us to help build up our wedding fund. I thought a celebration was called for, and offered to spring for milkshakes at the Dairy Thing.

Seemed to me the time had come to pop the question to Laurie, formal-like, but that's a story for another time.

# 5

# GRANNY AT THE LANDFILL

*by*

*Hunter Tydings*

Granny Frick's political career started at the landfill. I have to take some credit for that, since my exposé about the dump and its contents first appeared in the Rock Bottom Rambler. As editor of our weekly local paper, I see to it that front page news covers mostly automobile accidents, police activities, and School Board scandals. Once in a while a juicy story comes along, and I do what anyone in the journalism business does: I capitalize on the dirt and make it out to be the revelation of the century, enough scandal to hold the readers' interest for a week until they move on to another shocking local issue. Others in this business, however, do not have to deal with anyone like Granny Frick.

I learned from my sister-in-law's cousin that his uncle, Phil Boggs, who owns the land where the dump is located, was receiving truckloads of waste from other states in the middle of the night. Some waste disposal companies from New York and New Jersey were trucking tons of trash and garbage across several states and paying the landowner for the privilege of dumping the waste in our fair community, thereby putting our citizens in danger. There was a limit to how much we could deposit in that landfill, and it was supposed to take us over a hundred years to reach capacity. With the addition of out of state trash, we would exceed our limit in just a few years.

My editorial was the talk of Rock Bottom that week; most folks were outraged that the dumping was being allowed, but no one suggested a solution. A quick call to the Governor's office confirmed that he had given the go-ahead to sell rights to the landfill out of state, so I had no incentive to do any further legwork for in-depth coverage.

After reading the article, Miz Frick got so riled up she swung into action. Her son Emory took Granny to the site so she could see for herself what was going on. I have to admit that's more than I had done. The next thing I knew, Miz Frick had planted herself and a large drawstring garbage bag in the front office of the Rambler, and wouldn't budge until I agreed to hear her out. She ordered the receptionist to bring me out of hiding, or she would spend the night there. Her persistence, plus the fact that Emory was spitting sunflower shells all over the reception area, convinced me to meet with her. A noticeable aroma of landfill wafted around the old gal, proof she had been throwing herself into her latest project. She pulled herself up proudly to all of her 5 feet 2 inches.

"Hunter," she began, "I've known you all your life, and even changed your diapers a time or two!" Why do older ladies always have to point that out? Does that establish a natural dominion over me, just because she wiped my butt? "I have to congratulate you on a fine piece of work, boy. You have revealed a terrible wrong that needs to be made right, and I'm here to help you with the job."

"Well, Miz Frick - Granny - I do thank you for your kind compliment, and appreciate your offer to help, but I really don't see how we can do anything more…" I had published the editorial just to make a stir for one week, and had never intended to follow through; the judging of the annual Miss Ramp Contest was a more appealing pursuit.

Granny would not hear any arguments about ignoring the out of state dumping. It has been my experience that she is a force of nature, and when she sets her mind on something there's no stopping her. Lips set and eyes shooting sparks, Miz Frick gestured dramatically to the lumpy garbage bag she had brought with her.

"Take a look in there, sonny," she said, pointing with a gnarly finger and nodding her blue curls vigorously, "and you'll find something that will make your next week's headlines!"

Gingerly I opened the bag and fished out a few items on top of the heap of trash she had found at the dump. I recoiled and almost dropped the bag when I caught a glimpse of the universal hazard sign for radioactive waste. We emptied the whole bag onto newspapers and out spilled alarming things: containers with poison warnings, and more radioactive signs. Granny was right; this story would be even bigger than the one about the preacher who was arrested for bigamy last year. My jaw dropped as I looked at Miz Frick with new appreciation.

With a look of triumph, punctuated by a stomp of her sneaker, Granny Frick brushed off her gingham skirt and said, "Hunter, we've got some work to do! You'd best find out who's in on the profits when Phil Boggs lets them fellas from New York dump their garbage in this town, and why that stuff is allowed to poison our ground when other states have laws against it."

Picking up on her enthusiasm, I said to Granny, "Yes, and I need to find out where the hazardous waste comes from; and who owns those waste disposal companies; and why the town council is so quiet about this outrage?"

"There, that's the spirit!" shouted Granny, with a whack on my arm. "You are a fine young fella, and together we are going to take care of these upstarts from other states who think they can come here and take advantage of us folks in Rock Bottom. Ain't that right, Emory?" With that, she thumped Emory's arm, too, and sunflower seeds flew all over the new reception room rug. "I'll get folks together to rally at the dump, Hunter, and I'll talk to Sheriff Jim Purgitt. He ought to know we're about to take the law into our own hands unless his men can do it first. You visit the Mayor and Phil Boggs. We're going to get to the bottom of this."

I immediately caught on to the significance of our mission and saw visions of fame for the Rock Bottom Rambler and prosperity for me. Organizing a protest at the landfill and taking on big companies in states like New York and New Jersey could make statewide - even nationwide - headlines. Maybe offers for prestigious positions would pour in from The Washington Post, the Fresno Bee, or USA Today. My motivations for pursuing this investigation were not all selfish, of course; it surely was a travesty that the Rock Bottom landfill was being used cynically by powerful people in other states, with the cooperation of unscrupulous local opportunists and permission from the Governor.

I thanked Miz Frick for volunteering to help with this important breaking news story, and assured her we would work closely together on this project. It couldn't hurt my career to have it known that I was sharing my talents and fame with a little old lady who used to diaper me. Human interest stories always impress the readers. I owed my new fervor to Granny's determination and take-charge attitude, and the evidence she dumped onto my office carpet. I told the receptionist to admit Granny to my office at all times, but to discourage Emory with his proclivity for sunflower seeds.

My first interview was with Phil Boggs; since he was almost kin, it seemed only right to give him a chance to defend himself before I pilloried him in the Rambler. Stopping at the Bullseye on the way, I drove the five jarring miles up the rutted dirt road to his single-wide parked a hundred yards downwind of the landfill. Four scroungy dogs of questionable lineage greeted me with varying degrees of hostility. One had an injured voice box, so he could not bark, but made the motions anyway, whipping his head back and forth silently while he bared his teeth and opened and closed his jaws.

Checking the newly-purchased tape recorder in my pocket, I sauntered over to the ratty stuffed outdoor sofa where Phil was lounging. "Hey, there, Phil," I said with more friendliness than I felt, "how's life treating you?"

Phil took time to spit a mouthful of brown tobacco juice at the dogs, who grumbled and moved back, plopping down in the dust and snapping at their fleas and each other. "Just fine, Hunter; couldn't be better. Never thought I'd see the day when you'd come calling. Guess you're wanting to grill me about this here dump."

"You know how it is, Phil. Folks get their dander up and want answers. Bet you've made a sweet deal on this landfill thing, and they're all just envious."

Phil brightened up and gave another satisfied spit. "You just hit the nail on the head, Hunter. Every busybody in town would like to have a piece of the contract I have with Hasty Waste Disposal Company. I'm gonna be a rich man; then we'll see how uppity them folks will be. I'll be able to buy and sell all of them." He grinned a jack-o-lantern smile and kicked at one of the fleabags.

"Care to show me around, Phil? I'm real impressed with the operation you have here."

"That nosy old biddy, Emma Frick, already been here. Said she wanted to see for herself what the fuss was all about. Guess she was impressed, too."

Phil heaved himself out of the cushions and we trudged through foul-smelling piles of other people's waste. "What's that?" I asked, pointing to hazardous and radiation cautionary symbols.

"Aw, that ain't nothing," Phil said, "just some hospital stuff. The fellas from Hasty Waste told me they was hired to get rid of it 'cause no one in their states would let them dump it in a landfill. They 'pear to be really fine folks; theirs is a family business. Got a sense of humor, too; they even joked that they'd never put the bodies here! Ain't that a hoot?" Phil punctuated this with another spit and a cackle.

"How does the Mayor feel about this arrangement, Phil? Aren't you afraid the law will come after you for illegal dumping?"

"Hell, no, Hunter. I'm in good shape. The Mayor and me are business partners; he introduced me to these fellas, and we share the profits. Pretty good, huh? He got the Town Council to draw up a proposal for the Governor's office, which has got to give the go-ahead for such things."

"Got to hand it to you, Phil, you're going places." I didn't indicate exactly where Phil was headed. I thanked him for his time, wished him well, and waded back to my car through piles of trash and four angry dogs.

My next stop was the Mayor's office. Since I gave him good press in the Rambler during his campaign, Mayor Jackson "Bull" Schitz always makes time for me whenever I need to interview him. Ida the receptionist knows this and never gives me a hard time when I walk in unannounced. It doesn't hurt that I am always armed with either chocolates or flowers. She looked up from her game of computer solitaire and frowned.

"Uh, Hunter, the Mayor's tied up today. Sorry. Lemme make an appointment for you." Ida pretended to flip through the calendar. I tossed the box of candy at her desk so hard that it popped open and bonbons rolled across the desk and dropped to the floor. Poor Ida, bulky as she was, dove under her desk and frantically gathered candy. Taking advantage of her awkward position, I said, "You're welcome!" and bolted for Jackson's - Bull's - office. I really should have called ahead, because Bull was a busy man, shaving with a cordless electric while admiring himself in a propped-up desk mirror. His computer sported a dancing nude screensaver. I turned the recorder on again.

"Like what you see, Bull? Maybe getting ready for your appointment with a TV crew at the Sheriff's office?"

The Mayor jumped a couple inches out of his padded leather chair. "Hunter? What the hell are you doing here?"

"Nice to see you, too, Jackson." I laid a copy of the recent Rock Bottom Rambler under his nose and slammed it with my hand. "Don't tell me you haven't read my editorial yet. Why has the town not heard any comment from you? No cries of righteous wrath, no promises to investigate and stop this illegal dumping in our community?

Bull was no fool, I'll give him that. He smirked and leaned toward me, "No one interviewed me or asked my opinion about the problem, that's why. If you had done your job you would have asked my side of the story. So far no one in this pitiful town has even thought there might be a connection between me and Phil Boggs and the waste company filling our dump from out of state."

The cold truth was that the Mayor was right; I had a tip on what could be a regional scandal, and I had been too lazy to follow through on the first half-hearted attempt at an exposé. Then Granny Frick woke me up. I rallied and said, "I'm asking you now, Bull, to come clean and answer to the citizens you are bound to represent. I did my part to help elect you, and you at least owe me that."

"The way it looks to me, Hunter," sneered the Mayor, "you have two choices: you overlook this minor situation and we will cut you in on the profits, or you create an issue and you will find yourself and your weekly rag out of business and possibly in more hot water than you ever thought possible. These fellas from Jersey and New York are not real sociable. Besides, even if folks learn the whole truth, I'll tell them the money from this deal will fund a new park for the community; then we'll see how long their anger will last."

I felt oddly elated, as if for the first time in my life I knew I was doing the right thing in spite of possible loss of fortune, reputation and even safety, and it only reinforced my determination to go forward with the exposé. I had both Phil and Jackson on tape admitting to collusion in this illegal activity; even if we couldn't use the tapes, they would point the way to where to carry the investigation.

Just as I was going to strike back at Bull, we heard a commotion outside the office. It sounded like half the town was chanting outside the Mayor's window, and there was some scuffling in the reception area. The sound of trucks' horns blaring almost drowned out the angry voices.

Emma Frick called from the outer office, "Jackson Schitz, you varmint! Come out here and explain yourself. This here is one of your constipulents, and I want an accounting."

From the window, we could see that the crowd gathered outside the building had grown to a mob, and the chanting was louder: "Stop the trash trucks!" "Dump the Mayor!" "Let's talk trash!"

Bull looked panicked, and picked up the phone. Glaring at me, he snapped, "This is all your fault, Hunter! I'm calling the sheriff to remove these - these - *people* from the premises."

"Too late, Jackson," came a voice from the doorway. There stood Sheriff Purgitt with a scowling Granny Frick planted next to his elbow. Her frizzy head came almost up to his shoulder. He said, very coldly, "These...*people*...are citizens of this here town, and they got a right to assemble in a peaceful demonstration."

"Hear that, you weasel?" squawked Granny, "It ain't over yet! We're all going to the landfill to put a stop to the illegal dumping, and you and Phil Boggs and any other felon that's in on this scheme is going to jail."

The Sheriff continued, "I questioned your 'business partner,' and he caved in like the worthless coward he is. The Town Council admitted you forced them to falsify information on the proposal for the Governor. You threatened them with losing their jobs and their standing in the community."

Just then a pretty little gal pushed her way into the room, right next to Miz Frick. I recognized her after a minute of recollecting, but it had been many years since I had seen Granny's daughter, Irma Jean Beck. She seemed to have grown more attractive, and more noticeable in an intangible way. Irma Jean always used to be on the shy side and would not assert herself, especially during her marriage to that good-for-nothing husband. What hit me most, though, was the combination of hurt and determination in her eyes; silk and steel, I thought, and experienced an unexplainable desire to touch her soft brown hair. Landfill, scandal and weekly newspaper faded in importance while I tried to think of a way to impress Irma Jean.

"Well, Hunter?" said Granny, poking me hard, "are you with us? Wake up! We're heading over there now, and the boys is going to join us."

"What...what about you, Irma Jean?" I stammered, feeling like a foolish schoolboy.

"Of course, Mr. Tydings. This here is an unfair situation, and I want to help Maw make it right." No more mousy Irma Jean. Now she had some vinegar in her veins, and sort of reminded me what her Maw must have been like in her younger days, only Irma Jean was more attractive. She still showed a vulnerability that made me want to go along to protect her. "Sheriff," said Irma Jean, "these trash disposal outlaws show up in Rock Bottom every Thursday night. We citizens are going to be there to head them off tonight. Can we count on our law officers to protect us from the crooks who are about to violate our land and persons?"

Spunky gal!

Sheriff Purgitt hesitated only a split second before he agreed. "My deputies and me'll stake out the road at each end of town, and when them trucks show up we'll call ahead to warn you folks they're coming in. First, though, I'm gonna arrest this here Mayor, and the rest of the scum before they can warn the trash folks."

Granny Frick whooped, "That's the way to go, Jim Purgitt! I'll bring Ol' Betsy and my three boys, and we'll show those buzzards they can't push this town around!"

"Go easy, now, Miz Frick," warned the Sheriff, "don't you go doing anything unlawful, you hear? Leave Ol' Betsy at home, and keep them boys of yours on a tight leash."

The seed-spitting Emory and his two brothers, Radcliffe and Duke, were an unholy trio that only their Maw could keep in hand. It was my guess that the trash truck drivers would be lucky to get away from Rock Bottom in one piece, and then they'd never come back. Ol' Betsy was an ancient double-barrel shotgun that Granny has been known to use effectively, at least when she remembers to wear her specs. The thought of her swinging it around in the middle of the night at a landfill was enough to give me pause. Another reason to go along to protect Irma Jean.

"You stay with me, Irma Jean," I said. "It could get dangerous out there."

She said, "I'll do that, Mr. Tydings, but everything will be just fine. We're doing the right thing."

"Call me Hunter," I blurted.

Irma Jean just smiled, and I felt oddly young and silly.

Sheriff Purgitt took Bull Schitz away, and sent his deputies to pick up Phil Boggs and the Town Council. The rest of us formed into a small army of citizens with a mission. A motley assortment of

Rock Bottom's best set out for the landfill in pickups and on foot, chanting and hollering, carrying misspelled homemade signs. I did not even have to take notes for the editorial I was going to publish the next week; we were all living and making the news ourselves, and it gave us a feeling of empowerment like I'd never felt before.

There was only one dirt road leading into the landfill site, so we all lined up along the paved county route and blocked access to the dump. Granny Frick was in the forefront of the organizing and cheerleading, getting everyone riled up. Local high school kids showed up, and their teachers did, too. I recognized Charlene and her friends from the Budz, a dancing club that most of us men folk knew about; I saw no reason to enlighten Irma Jean or her Maw about who they were. Folks from the plant came when their shifts let out, and ladies came straight from the beauty salon. Some Methodists showed up on the flatbed of a pickup and inspired us all with hymns like *Onward, Christian Soldiers.* Most touching of all was the contingent of mountain men who came down from the hills to stand with us in solidarity; they stood apart, silent and dark, with wolf-like eyes that watched and glittered. Their stride was smooth and measured like a panther's, and they wore buckskins with knives strapped to their legs. Nothing had ever brought them out of their hills to mingle with town folks before, and everyone was real impressed and maybe a little scared.

Granny's sons Emory and Duke got a bonfire going; I think maybe Duke was a little too eager to watch something burn, but the fire was cheery and got everyone in the right mood of defiance and patriotism. Their brother Radcliffe - known as Cliff - showed up with a surprise for Miz Frick. He had gone to the next county to enlist Granny's favorite country singers, Bucky Burke and the Bail-Jumpers, to perform while folks waited for the trash trucks to show up. Cliff the entrepreneur also provided the excited crowd with his home-brewed liquid refreshment. The Methodists and the gals from the Beehive beauty salon brought eats for everybody. We roasted hot dogs and marshmallows over the Frick boys' fire, and sang along with the Bail-Jumpers. Charlene and the other girls raised morale in their own way when Granny wasn't looking.

Irma Jean and I got to know each other better, and I was more and more impressed with her. I had no idea if she liked me or not, but she did give a little mysterious smile several times, and she never told me to buzz off. The evening was like a huge block party, and until the Sheriff called we were having a wonderful time and forgot why we were there.

My cell phone rang at about 1:00 a.m., and suddenly everything got dead quiet. In the distance we heard the labored growl of big overloaded trucks making their way up the grade. The crowd drew together and closed ranks. When the waste disposal trucks came around the last bend and into our sight, they faced an angry silent bunch of citizens who meant business. Miz Frick, as spokesman for the group, stepped forward and challenged the first driver. I noticed she had brought her specs with her.

"Turn your rig around and go back where you came from, sonny. This here is Rock Bottom, and we don't take no trash from other states!"

"Get out of the way, sister," snarled the driver in a funny accent, "if you don't want to get run over. We got a job to do and you and your redneck friends aren't going to stop us."

"Oh, yes, we are!" called out Irma Jean.

The mob surged forward behind her and surrounded the truck. The noise of the crowd nearly drowned out the roar of the trucks. The drivers put their rigs in gear and started to move forward with no regard for the safety of anyone, women or old folks alike, standing in the way, and crashed into the barriers people had set up across the landfill road. Quick as foxes, two of the mountain men jumped onto each of the two trucks and grabbed onto the steering wheels. In very low and level voices they said, "You really don't want to come any closer, now, DO you?" All the while their predator eyes bored into the drivers.

Just then the Sheriff from one direction, and his deputies from the other, converged on the landfill. With guns drawn, they confronted the drivers and convinced them to turn around and head back. Later on, some folks swore there were shots fired from the crowd, but no one owned up to having a weapon there. One truck appeared to have 00 buckshot holes in the door just where the driver's butt would be; the law did not seem eager to investigate. No one has seen the trucks since, and no more garbage from out of state has been dumped in our fair town.

The Rock Bottom Rambler won statewide honors for its exclusive coverage of the trash dumping scandal, and our circulation increased into the tri-county region. It was a shame to see Irma Jean's talent and good sense wasted on a factory job, so I hired her to do local reporting for the paper. Her chief sources of tips are her Maw and the girls at the Beehive beauty salon. Naturally, Irma Jean and I have to spend a lot of overtime at the paper, and we make a good team. With the increased revenue I established an internship for young aspiring journalists, and the first spot was awarded to Caltech Beck, Irma Jean's son, a fine young man who has been studying Criminology at Tech. He plans to combine the internship and the study of Criminology to pursue a career in investigative journalism. His Granny will be real proud.

The Governor remained beyond reach of the law because it could be proven that he was hoodwinked by the Town Council's falsified proposal. The citizens, however, had their doubts, and a statewide campaign to unseat him resulted in the Governor being voted out of office in the next election. Our town capitalized on the publicity by turning the landfill into a tourist attraction of sorts, and charging a small fee for admission. The signs at the entrance to Rock Bottom read, "Site of the Famous Landfill Protest" and "Birthplace of Emma Frick". The profits were used to build a new athletic field for the Rock Bottom Hellbenders.

"Most important," said Granny, "is that Rock Bottom can trash its own land in peace."

The arrests and convictions of the corrupt members of the town government left a vacuum, and that's how Granny Frick began her political career. By popular acclamation she ran for office, but that is another story, and the Rambler is following it closely.

# 6

# GRANNY RUNS FOR OFFICE

*by*

*Wheeler Diehl*

As a member of the Rock Bottom Town Council, I wish I could take credit for Emma "Granny" Frick's foray into the world of local politics. The truth is that a motley assortment of Rock Bottom citizens began a movement to elect Granny to the Mayor's office by popular acclaim. Miz Frick had the support of the Rock Bottom Rambler, a populist base, and a cause that energized voters like no other ever had. This wiry, rumpled old gal was an unstoppable force with sharp eyes that didn't miss a thing, and flyaway hair that made a statement of refusal to be bound by convention. Her signature attire was shapeless sweaters and high-top tennis shoes.

The Rambler had broken the story about out-of-state companies using Cornrow County land to dump their hazardous waste. Granny and the editor of the newspaper organized a protest that drove the waste truckers out of town and stopped the illegal dumping. She probably didn't realize that she was opening a can of worms. The big shake-up, now referred to as The Landfill Massacre, forced the Mayor and most of the Town Council to resign, and because of the suspicion that his involvement in the scheme was greater than he admitted, even the Governor lost his bid for reelection

I was the only Councilman to survive the Massacre; I happened to be out of town when the landfill business was brought before the Council, and didn't participate in the debate or the vote. My political enemies put out scurrilous reports that I was in the Bahamas with my girl friend. I squelched those rumors before the special election. The folks hereabouts have no concept of geography, so no one has looked into Bermuda. My wife does her thing and I do mine. I let her live in style to keep her happy. She will vouch for me because she has her eye on the Governorship for me someday, and maybe national office after that. It doesn't hurt that the new governor is her uncle.

If I do run for statewide office, I must utilize the enthusiasm and energy of the Granny crowd. Her enthusiastic supporters ran the chaotic campaign in a state of emotional abandon. They disrupted traffic flow to hand out fliers that said, "Frick is our Pick". They put up posters in local shop windows, "Bust Your Fanny to Vote for Granny", and they gave out souvenir underwear with the imprint, "I Support Granny Frick". To raise money for the impromptu campaign, Miz Frick's fans held bake sales on sidewalks and Bingo games in the Fire Hall ("We'll Hit the Jackpot with Emma Frick"). They raffled off some of her renowned homemade pies, and she autographed photos of herself holding Ol' Betsy the shotgun. The proprietor of the Beehive Beauty Salon sold snips of Granny's hair as souvenirs. Rumor has it that some of the locks were fake because they were red, and everyone knew Granny wouldn't ever let dye touch her hair.

Picture, if you can, the spectacle of the neophyte candidate on the flatbed of her son's truck, waving to her rabid supporters as she stumped from one end of Rock Bottom to the other. Anywhere in Rock Bottom is within walking distance of any other part of town, but the rattletrap old truck was a statement not lost on the citizens. It was a circus worthy of the National Convention of a major party. Folks of every description marched along, cheering, and carrying flags and balloons. The band from Rock Bottom High School's Hellbenders led the way, playing *Happy Days Are Here Again* and *The Battle of New Orleans.*

Gals that some of us knew as Peaches and Honeydew, and a couple of their associates, all working under different stage names now, marched along throwing kisses to the crowd. I held Berry (can't recollect what she calls herself now) at bay when she ran up to me on the sidelines saying, "Hey, Sugar! We getting together Friday night?"

"Hush up, sweetheart," I muttered, looking around to see who noticed, "not in public!" I had to maintain a modicum of uprightness for the time being. If my colleagues and I were going to stop the Granny train, we had work to do.

As the local politicians discovered, however, no matter what any of the parties - Democrat, Republican, or Fringe Party - did to stop Emma Frick's candidacy, it didn't work. They put out reports about her connections with drug dealers, flimflam artists, and illegal producers of hooch. The charges didn't sway public opinion since most of these perpetrators of petty crimes had been either local crooks she brought to justice, or her relatives, who were no longer involved in these illegal pursuits.

Everyone jumped onto the Granny bandwagon. Older people supported her because she wasn't young; young people liked her because she stood up to the establishment. Independents liked her because she was a registered Independent; Democrats and Republicans tolerated her because she didn't belong to That Other Party. Poor folks adored her because she was honest and spoke up for them. The well-heeled respected her because she bluntly blackmailed them into funding her favorite causes, and they all wanted in return a good word on their behalf and flattering photos in the Rambler. Church ladies sang her praises because she fought for public morality; local strippers rallied to her because she looked the other way, up to a point.

No one could succeed in Rock Bottom politics after The Landfill Massacre unless he stepped into line with Granny. Being no dummy, I knew which way to lean.

There were two other half-hearted candidates who wanted Rock Bottom to have a rational choice, so they set up a debate in the back room of Ernie's Garden Supplies. Hubert Weezle, a minor Republican player, was Assistant Manager of Rock Bottom's largest (and only) bank, Foreclosures United Bank, or F. U. Bank for short. His campaign was funded by the bank and by his Daddy, a Deacon at the Joyful Noise Church.

The other candidate was Ethan "Dizzy" Rambeau, a wild-eyed member of the Fringe Party. He was Maintenance Engineer at the Cornrow County rehab facility, and part-owner of a taxidermy business. No one seemed to know what the Fringe Party stood for; no one was courageous enough to question the party members.

Democrats didn't even try to take the election away from Granny Frick. Her supporter base was the same as theirs, so they would only split the vote between them, leaving the Republican or – heaven help us – the Fringe Party to win the Mayor's office.

The evening of the debate rolled around. Red and blue lights played on the sheeting stapled to the ceiling. Red, white and blue balloons broke free from their moorings and occasionally popped with a bang when they brushed up against Ernie's hot gel lights. The regional TV news channel sent a curvy reporter with low-cut bodice, and a tobacco-chewing cameraman. A reporter from the Rambler showed up to cover the event, but Miz Frick's opponents cried foul; the reporter was Irma Jean Beck, her daughter. The monitor of the debate was Hunter Tydings, editor of the Rambler. Once again, it seemed to be a set-up because Hunter and Granny together had exposed the landfill scandal, and he was currently dating Irma Jean.

Rather than face the ire of the Rock Bottom mob that constituted Granny's voters, her opponents reluctantly agreed to go ahead with the debate. Hunter Tydings read the rules of the evening, which were simple: the first to speak would pose a two-minute question to his/her opponents, who would then have four minutes each to respond. The next candidate would then ask a question, and so forth.

The candidates drew straws, and the Republican went first. "Good evening, Miz Emma Frick, Mr. Rambeau, and Mr. Tydings. We find ourselves on the brink of a momentous election here in Rock Bottom, an election in which much is at stake for the citizens of this town, the county, and even the great state of…" Here he was interrupted by the moderator, Hunter Tydings.

"Mr. Weezle, I remind you that you have two minutes to ask your question. Please proceed in a timely manner."

"Very well. My first question concerns the plans for going forward in Rock Bottom. What do you see as priority programs for the welfare of our town? First, Miz Frick?"

The crowd that had pushed its way into Ernie's and was spilling out into the yard cheered and waved Granny signs.

"Please maintain order and silence," yelled the moderator, "or you will be asked to leave! Miz Frick, four minutes."

I was impressed that Hunter was trying to be impartial.

"Thanks, sonny." Granny smiled and waved at her supporters, who hooted louder and waved back.

Hunter punched the bell vigorously, and managed to bring the unruly horde under control.

Emma Frick put on her glasses and looked at some wrinkled wads of paper she fished out of her pocket. "This here's the report on the school system in Cornrow County. Funds that was earmarked by the state for our schools got stole by some members of the School Commission and used for contracts that was given to their relatives' companies at costs way higher than they should've been. My 'priority program', Mr. Weezle, would be: first, to fire all Commissioners who stole that money, and get the law after them; second, get rid of all contracts this county is paying for that wasn't bid on proper; and third, make the lowdown scallywags pay back out of their own profits the money they stole from the schools."

The place erupted in cheers and whistles, but Miz Frick calmed everyone down with a wave of her hand. "Next, we need to set up a place where the young folks can go to play games, eat snacks and meet their friends. Better than having them hanging around and breaking all ten of the Commandments.

"The library needs more reference books so's folks can look up what they need to know. They could also use a couple of them computers in the library, too, all wired up to that worldwide thing that everybody uses, and the young folks could use them for homework assignments."

The teenagers in the crowd went crazy, stomping and yelling, "Granny Rules!"

Granny continued, "The roads in Rock Bottom is a shame to the town, and our bridges is cracked and falling down. We need to do something about that. Seems to me the state can be persuaded to chip in some money for that, and the companies can bid, proper-like, so's we get the most reasonable deal."

The moderator signaled that time was up for Miz Frick, and told "Dizzy" Rambeau it was his turn to respond to Mr. Weezle's question.

It took a moment for Mr. Rambeau to focus, then he scratched his unruly mop of bristly hair and glared at the audience fiercely. "It's coming, y'all. The Revolution is closer than you think. Now's the time to join the Fringe Party! We got plans, and organization, and contacts. Our priority's got to be readiness for the takeover! We got to stockpile arms, get us some money, and get rid of our enemies who want to keep us down!" He was clenching the podium, and looking people in the eye; he seemed to burn with a fanatical fire. "There's a conspiracy afoot, my friends! We're onto them, and we're gonna make our move before they make theirs."

There was silence, except for a few stifled gasps.

All of a sudden, a balloon met its explosive end against a hot light with a bang that sent "Dizzy" Rambeau diving under the podium.

The TV cameraman hurried forward to catch the scene close-up, and a few in the audience squealed. The nubile reporter fluffed her hair, and spoke dramatically into her microphone,

"The debate in Rock Bottom's special mayoral election campaign has taken a nasty turn, with one candidate threatening to overturn the government. Shots have been fired."

Granny said in a low voice, "Now, Ethan, calm down. Have you taken your medicine today?"

"Dizzy" shook his head sheepishly as he crept out from under the podium. His hands and voice were shaking. "I done forgot, Miz Frick."

"I thought so, Ethan. We won't mind if you want to go home and take your meds and lie down for awhile; you'll feel much better."

With an agreeable nod, a small sob and a mumbled "OK", Mr. Rambeau took his leave and the debate continued.

Hunter, shaken by the outburst, recovered nicely. "Mr. Weezle, would you care to discuss your own priorities as Mayor, and respond to Miz Frick's proposed programs?"

Delighted to have the podium at last, Hubert Weezle stepped closer to the microphone. "Gladly, Mr. Tydings. It is an honor to be part of this historic debate in our fine town, and I thank you, sir, for generously agreeing to dedicate your evening as moderator." Small pause to assume a statesman-like pose. "My priority as Mayor will be to ferret out the businesses and individuals in Rock Bottom who arrogantly avoid paying their taxes. Scofflaws cost the rest of us a heavier burden of taxes to pay for the things the town needs. Secondly, I will continue the time-honored practice of granting contracts to the most successful and long-term members of the community whose quality of work is well known and reliable."

A heckler booed from the audience. "What you mean, Weezle, is that the good ol' boys who vote for you will get the best contracts from the town, then will do their usual below-standard work!"

Another voice was raised, "I'm tired of rescuing my chickens from a flood every time it rains because my street weren't graded right. The contractor was a relative of one of them Town Council Members. Another business with connections put the new roof on the courthouse, and now it's losing shingles every time a wind blows."

"Yeah, Hubert, the roofer was your brother-in-law! Shoot, I wonder how he got the contract? Maybe your position in F.U. Bank had something to do with that – did you promise loans to the Board members?"

Hubert Weezle looked desperately at Hunter Tydings and said, "Aren't you supposed to moderate this debate? The audience aren't supposed to put their two cents' worth in."

Hunter smiled slightly and said, "Hubert, I seem to have lost control here. This is all being filmed by the TV crew, so you can watch it over and over on the news."

Hubert got hot under the collar. "Fine! You people want all the nice toys and frills that Miz Frick is promising you. Recreation centers for kids! Computers in the library! How the hell do you think she's going to fund these projects? Huh? Think about that. Nobody wants more taxes, but they bring in revenue to make the town a better place. Miz Frick, I'm asking you directly, how do you plan to fund these unnecessary projects?"

The room erupted with angry shouts and boos, but the moderator did his job and banged on the bell until order was restored. "Miz Frick, You have four minutes to answer Mr. Weezle's question about the funding of your projects."

Granny tilted her head and pursed her lips as she pondered. Finally, she said, "Roads and bridges is a big project, for sure, and as I said before, we'll need state money for that. Seems to me we're due for our fair share. It was this town what uncovered the landfill scandal and got those varmints kicked out of office. If some of our citizens go to Capital City in a delegation, we can persuade the lawmakers there to vote us some funds. Better be sure, though, that we send only folks who clean up good and behave theirselves.

"As for the other stuff – books and computers for the library is going to be donated by companies and people I've already talked to. Whether or not I'm elected, these things are going to be given to Rock Bottom.

"The other project – a center for young folks – is easy enough. There's a building in town that has stood empty for the past four years. No one wants to buy it, and it's just collecting dust and mice. You know the building I'm talking about, Mr. Weezle, because it belongs to you: the old Holler Dollar store. In my plan you're going to be real generous and donate that old useless piece of real estate to the youngsters. For a tax break, of course."

Here Miz Frick was interrupted by applause from the youthful cheering section.

She continued, "The cleanup, repairs and painting can be done free by the young folks theirselves because they're the ones to get the benefit. Any materials needed can be paid for in three ways. First, Rock Bottom can have one extra gun bash every year, with profits going to pay for keeping up the Youth Center; folks from other towns and counties will bring money into Rock Bottom for a gun bash, guaranteed. Second, we have one of the best parks in the Tri-County region, and folks from all over comes here to have picnics, family gatherings and church socials. Rock Bottom could charge out-of-county visitors a little fee – say, one dollar for each car load – for a day's use of the park...."

Hunter Tydings broke in with a time warning, "Miz Frick, your time is almost up. You have thirty seconds to finish up."

Unperturbed, Granny continued, "Third, I never expected to run for Mayor or anything else, but the Good Lord has seen fit to put me here. The folks of this town been real generous with donations to this campaign, but truth be told, I ain't had to put up money for very much. I pledge all the extra money we ain't used in this run for office to be used for whatever the Youth Center needs; I ain't going to run again, so I won't need those funds for another campaign."

Just then the bell dinged and the place exploded with cheers. Weezle was speechless.

The moderator reminded Emma Frick, "You now have two minutes to ask your opponent a question, Miz Frick. Proceed."

She said, "Mr. Weezle, I want the folks to hear from you why you want to be Mayor, and what makes you think you deserve to be one?"

There was a stir in the audience. A sullen man with a week's growth of beard stood up and addressed the moderator. "Excuse me, Mr. Tydings. I'm a member of the Fringe Party, and our candidate had to leave the debate early for uh...health...reasons. I want to answer that question for him, since he ain't here to speak for hisself."

To his credit, Hunter handled the situation with diplomacy. "I don't think anyone here would object to your giving a four-minute answer on Mr. Rambeau's behalf. Please state your name, and affiliation with the absent candidate."

"My name don't matter none; I'm just a loyal member of the party what works closely with 'Dizzy' to get us freedom lovers ready for the struggle against tyranny. Mr. Rambeau wants to be Mayor to get the people ready for the takeover. We've had it with corruption and bureaucracy, and want to raise our party above and beyond all that."

A heckler called out, "In other words, you want to go beyond the fringe!"

Looking perplexed, the True Believer answered, "I guess you could say that. Mr. Rambeau – "Dizzy", as we affectionately refer to him – has learned organizational skills as Maintenance Engineer, cleaning up, so to speak. Taxidermy has taught him the patience and attention to detail he needs to accomplish long-term goals."

Heckler Number 2 yelled, "Tell that oddball to stuff it!"

Hunter tapped the bell. "I think that's enough. Mr. Weezle?"

"My qualifications need no elucidation, Mr. Tydings. As reported in your fine paper, I have been Assistant Manager of the Foreclosures United Bank…"

"F.U., Weezle!" This from another disgruntled member of the audience.

"…for six months, and as such have acquired the managerial and financial skills that will stand me in good stead as Mayor of Rock Bottom. Our bank listens to the customer, and as Mayor I will hear and answer all complaints and concerns of the citizens."

Speaking over the boos and jeers, the moderator passed the question along to Emma Frick.

"Well, sonny, I ain't got nothing to give folks excepting just me. I fight for what's right, just as we did at the landfill, and I want what's best for everybody, especially the youngsters what is the future of Rock Bottom."

Predictably, the place erupted with hullabaloo from Granny's fans. Weezle and Rambeau's flunky slunk away with their tails between their legs. I made a big show of congratulating Miz Frick on her outstanding performance in the debate, and shook her hand long enough for the press to take several photos. Funny she couldn't recall my name.

The Rambler gave the campaign and the debate several pages of coverage. They even splurged on color photos, and it wasn't even Gun Bash day. The paper's circulation skyrocketed that week; I suspect Irma Jean got a raise.

Miz Frick's adoring followers escorted her to the polls on special election day. She waved and smiled on her way into the booth, and gave a TV crew from Midville an interview outside the polling place. To everyone's surprise, Granny revealed she had not voted for herself. "That don't seem like the sporting thing to do. I voted for that poor befuddled, angry soul that probably got only a few votes."

The curvy young reporter said, "Oh, you mean Hubert Weezle?"

Emma Frick just smiled and moved on.

Granny's election as Mayor was headline news on TV and in the Rock Bottom Rambler for days. All her ragtag supporters were invited to her victory party. I forced my wife to attend, and asked my girl friend not to. The event featured Bucky Burke and the Bail-Jumpers, venison jerky, and punch that had a kick like a blind mule. Nearly everyone enjoyed the heady celebration, even though no shots were fired.

True to her campaign platform, Granny had the crooked Council members arrested and indicted; the progression of their trials remains front-page fodder for the Rock Bottom Rambler. The library now sports computers and new books, and the teenagers can raise hell in their own recreation center. All town contracts have to be bid on "proper", which is bad news for my excavating and septic system company. We'll bid low anyway, and make up the difference in below standard grade materials, the effects of which won't come to light until long after Granny leaves office. A feisty delegation led by Miz Frick besieged the State Government with demands for road and bridge repairs, and damned if they didn't get what they went after! That woman is persistent, I'll give her that.

Those of us elected to the new Town Council are, of course, grateful to have a job in these difficult economic times, but it is humiliating to be a rubber stamp for any wild plan Granny hatches. We have no choice but to go along with her harebrained schemes and ignorance of political procedures. Miz Frick promised not to run for a second term; I have to admit she is a woman of her word, so all I have to do is endure and plan. With an eye to my political future, I publicly support all of Miz Frick's programs enthusiastically. I embrace her constituency as my own, and cultivate every unshaven, incoherent voter who visits the Town Council offices with a petition.

Even those in the Fringe Party.

# 7

# GRANNY THE ARTIST

*by*

*Viola Haze*

Of all the art studios in the universe, Emma "Granny" Frick had to walk into mine. I am always happy to help prospective artists to, like, develop their talents and find their muse and all that, but this woman drove me to tranquillizers and, worse, to doubt in my own abilities as an artist and teacher. The first day we met was a pastel spring day with the sweet scent of clover in the air. Ms. Frick stood in the door of my studio smoking a cigarette. Okay, I have no problem with a smoke now and then - I even roll my own papers – but her smoke smelled foul, like trash burning. I suspect her brand was a very cheap one, such as Cold Goats. Being around her for long would activate a headache.

Ms. Frick was wearing a gray sweater, rumpled calico skirt and tennis shoes. Although I got a good vibe from her attire, I sensed that she and I would have little in common beyond our mutual good taste in clothing.

I said, "May I help you, ma'am? Do you need directions?"

"Nope," she replied, "I'm just where I want to be. This here is the Purple Palette Art Studio and Gallery, ain't it?"

"This is it. Do you want to buy some of the students' work on display? Our monthly theme is '*Cicadas in Ballet*'. So avant garde, so happening!"

"Missy, I didn't understand any of what you was talking about. I come here to take art lessons. I have a hankering to paint something."

Shaken at the thought of having to teach this tacky person the fine art of painting, I asked if she had any previous artistic training.

"Only in eighth grade; took Arts and Crafts for a semester until the teacher made me quit."

I could see that my abilities were going to be challenged, and I had enough problems of my own. A headache, now full-blown and throbbing, made me want a cup of herbal tea. I frowned and rubbed my forehead.

"Missy, I know what's good for a headache."

"I'm sorry. What did you say?" I mumbled.

"A nice cup of tea will work wonders for a headache. I see a kettle on the burner over there; you set yourself down and relax. I'll fix you a cup."

Flustered at the unexpected attention from this strange woman, I blurted out a thank you and sat down on the hammock.

"I'm Emma Frick, but you can call me Granny. Us artists got to stick together. Mind if I join you in a cup of tea?" She smacked her lips approvingly. "That there's a good yarbal tea; could use a drop of spirits to liven it up a bit. You know, you're way too thin, Miz…"

"Uh, Haze, Viola Haze."

"Miz Haze Viola Haze, you need some meat on your bones! If you're not eating well, that'll give a body headaches for sure." How did she guess? I couldn't afford to pay my studio rent, much less buy enough food to keep hunger at bay. "I've been too busy to – uh – like, fix meals, okay?"

After sipping and relaxing, I asked, "Do you have any samples of your work, Ms. Frick – Granny?"

"Nothing I can carry around with me. I'm real proud of my squash and watermelons, and my pies can't be beat."

"I mean, any artwork, like, sketches or paintings?"

"Oh, that. Not yet, but I can whip up a few and bring them back in a few days. When do the lessons start?"

"W-well, you see…" I stammered, "I have to assess your abilities and place you in just the right class for your level of progress. I have beginners; those who have progressed somewhat; and the most proficient students, who are entitled to show their work in the gallery and offer them for sale."

"I seen them pictures in the gallery, Miz Haze, and I tell you what, I can't make heads or tails out of them. You ever sell any?"

"Yes, of course; in fact, we, uh, sold one…one just last week," I lied. Well, it wasn't exactly a lie; my father had passed through town and out of pity for the struggling gallery, he bought *Cicada Pas de Deux*. It was priced at $350.00, but he gave me $200.00 for it; said he couldn't make heads or tails out of it. Dad has a good heart, but no artistic discernment.

"Missy, let me give you some advice," said Granny, "and I mean this in a nice way. You can increase sales in this here town if you and your students paint pictures what look like everyday things folks see right here in Rock Bottom. Take these ones you got on display now. 'Cicadas in Ballet', my foot. They don't look like bugs or ballet dancers, Viola; they're just blotches and splashes of ugly colors that wouldn't even match anybody's wallpaper or furniture covers."

Her impressions were predictably banal, but now that my headache had passed I was ready to take on a challenge. "I can't answer that in any way you would understand. Art is not about representation, but about feelings, or impressions, or essence. Please do come and take lessons here, and I will transform your perceptions from the mundane to the transcendent."

"You can transform away, Missy, but life is also about keeping body and soul together. Instead of going hungry with bugs and ballet, you could bring in enough cash to ease your mind and pay the bills."

Oh, the seduction of base lucre! How many great artists have succumbed to the allure of mammon? How many have sold their artistic integrity for a square meal? The answer is: many.

How many have given up their dreams of fame in New York City and settled for the likes of Rock Bottom? Well, that's one for sure.

"Ms. Frick, I'll agree to give you lessons if you will agree to keep an open mind about letting the muse lead you where it will. You can paint all the green tractors and fuzzy kittens you like at first, then we will see where your talent takes you."

Granny slapped her leg. "It's a deal, Viola!" she yelped. "We'll get this here gallery running in the black in no time."

"Cool! And you, Ms. Frick, will encounter a new world of creativity beyond your wildest dreams."

Since Granny's budget would allow for only one lesson per week, I placed her in the Tuesday beginner class, with unlimited access to the studio for practice. We started the classes with the basics: shapes, perspective, shading, light source. We drew from three dimensional shapes and vases of flowers. We went outside and drew from nature: landscapes, trees, cows grazing. We drew pictures of each other and of famous people, while assuring Granny that "we ain't going to paint no naked hussies". Granny seemed to defy the concepts, and her presentation was shocking. I would have to describe her style as belonging to the coloring book school of art. She favored flat expanses of primary color, outlined heavily in black. A tree was most definitely nothing but a tree to Granny, and she drew it as a brown stick topped by a green splotch, with no personality or depth. The sky was always blue, and a bright yellow sun (outlined in black, of course) always shone overhead. Compared to Granny, the other beginning students were budding Rembrandts. They were kind enough not to laugh at her outright, but her paintings elicited raised eyebrows and mumbled exclamations. My intake of tranquillizers increased.

Exasperated, I could stand it no longer. "Ms. Frick, have you ever really looked at a tree? Have you observed that the branches spread out in different directions, and that roots anchor the tree to the ground? Some trees bear fruit, and some have moss on the bark. They have shadows and texture that give them dimension, and their leaves and branches move and bend in the wind. In other words, they have soul."

"You don't have to tell me about trees, Missy," said Granny, "I know where they grow and which ones burn best in a wood stove. Some is good for shade, and others give syrup in the spring. Ain't never seen no soul, but I know what a picture of a tree should look like. It should be easy to tell it's a tree, and leave no questions about whether it's this or that kind – just a tree."

With a flash of insight, I exclaimed, "Oh, groovy! I understand! You are painting the essence of a tree – a tree reduced to its most basic form. You are indeed growing and opening up to the muse, Granny!"

"If you say so, Viola. If this muse fella shows up, let him in and I'll ask him to buy a couple of paintings."

As the weeks rolled by, Granny's paintings took on a more controlled style, albeit naïve and primitive. There was no doubt that her fields of corn were just that, and people, trees, animals and barns marched from bottom to top of the canvas with total lack of perspective. I was often on the verge of breaking out into tears or hives. This was my first complete failure at teaching the rudiments of art. My students usually go away satisfied with their progress, and with a few minimally awful paintings to show for their time and effort. Not even the tranquillizers worked any more.

On Friday afternoons I do not hold classes, which gives me a chance to chill out, do my own thing, and figure out how I'm going to pay next month's rent. Maybe Daddy needs another painting. One Friday, I had just put a relaxing ocean sound CD in my player and lit some aromatherapy candles, when the knock on the door came. Surprised, I opened the door to find Granny standing there looking tickled pink. Behind her was a derelict pickup truck loaded with stacks of framed paintings. One of her idiot sons sat grinning in the driver's seat. The headache started.

"Well, Viola, I'm ready to make the Purple Palette famous. Ain't that good news? Got four dozen of my best paintings in the truck, and Emory's going to help us hang them in the gallery."

"Ms. Frick – Granny – I don't know what to say."

"Shoot, you don't have to thank me. Emory made the frames hisself, so they didn't cost much. We tore down an old outhouse for the wood."

I was rubbing my throbbing head.

"Missy, you're so excited you've worked yourself up into another one of them headaches, ain't you? Let's sit down and have a cup of tea while Emory brings the paintings in. We have to work out how much to ask for these here pictures, and how much commission you're going to charge."

I stopped shaking long enough to collapse on the hammock while Granny prepared tea and her son brought in the paintings.

Emory said, "Ain't these paintings a sight?"

I had to agree they were a sight.

"We're all real proud of Maw. She's the first Frick to hang in a gallery. There was another Frick, a long time ago, who was hanged and..."

"Hush up, Emory!" Granny snapped. "That was different."

"These here paintings of Maw's is going to make your gallery lots of money, Miss."

The paintings showed a predictable assortment of commonplace subjects: flowers, birds, barns, children on playgrounds, wild animals, farm animals, and huge watermelons and squash. All were done in large splashes of primary colors, outlined in black, with Granny's signature, EFrick, written in bold but shaky lines across the lower edge of the canvas. The overall effect was appalling, but crazily consistent.

I was too defeated to stand up to them. "I can only say I'm – overcome. This is more than I ever bargained for – uh, hoped for."

With a triumphant smile, Granny said, "And here's the most exciting part, Viola. Hunter Tydings is going to feature the gallery, and my paintings, in the Rock Bottom Rambler. That will be a lot of free publicity for you. He's engaged to my daughter, so he's happy to help in any way."

I lost it. I collapsed, sobbing, "Oh, no! Not publicity! What am I going to do? I'll have to move to another town, another state; maybe even to Canada. How will I ever face my peers?"

Granny tried to console me. "If you're worried about trying to handle all the new customers, just relax and let me and Emory take care of them for you. All you'll have to do is stroll through the gallery with flowers in your hair and smile real sweet and dreamy like you do, and we'll answer questions and take their money. Hmmm. We could even make a little extra by selling cups of that yarbal tea and some of them brownies you and your friends call magic."

The thought of this gallery making money by selling herbal tea and magic brownies to the denizens of Rock Bottom struck me as being so hilarious that I went from convulsive sobs to racking laughter. Granny and her dense son mistook my hysteria for wholehearted approval, and the three of us laughed ourselves silly.

"You win, I give up," I gasped between giggles. "Do whatever you like, Granny; I'm at your mercy. I'm headed for bankruptcy anyway; might as well go down as comic relief."

So it happened that the Purple Palette was the chosen venue for the artistic debut of Emma Frick, who titled the exhibit *Rock Bottom: Nowhere to Go but Up*. We had a reception on the opening evening. Granny's oldest son wanted to provide home brew, but the Rambler came to the rescue and spotted us the money for drinks and refreshments. Hunter Tydings strong-armed some local bigwigs to attend. He assured them that their presence at a cultural event would win them votes in the next election, or increase sales in their family businesses.

Granny showed up in her Sunday best, with freshly "blued" hair. She complained that the punch lacked some kick, and added something to it from a jar she produced from her tote bag. The resulting "kick" was greatly appreciated by the guests, and we had to refill the bowl several times during the evening.

"What the heck are these silly little sandwiches?" complained Granny. "They ain't big enough to keep a bird fed, and they have odd pasty fillings I ain't never et before."

I noticed, however, that she scooped up a dozen or so and stashed them in her tote bag for later.

The idiot son Emory cleaned up well, and looked almost dashing in the tux we rented for him. He made a good impression on female guests until he opened his mouth and spoke. I placed him at the door to help with wraps, but he kept wandering back to the punch bowl.

At Granny's suggestion, I dressed in something filmy and far-out (by Rock Bottom standards), and wore flowers braided into my hair. It was not difficult to act dreamy and disconnected, because I so did not want to be there. My level of embarrassment was tempered, however, when the comments from these small town Philistines were not only appreciative, but resulted in several sales. Emma Frick had driven a hard bargain: her paintings were to be offered at $350.00 apiece, the same as the works by more advanced students, but I had held out for thirty percent commission for myself. That night we sold ten paintings; tomorrow I could pay the rent and eat.

The local paper did a two-page spread on the studio, the gallery and the exhibit, complete with photos of some of Granny Frick's best work. It wasn't long before other papers in the Tri-County area picked up the story and ran it. Suddenly, EFrick originals were in demand, and as soon as they sold Granny would turn out more to replace them. I added a new wing onto the gallery just for her paintings, with a media room and a gift shop where we sold souvenirs; anything to squeeze a dollar out of the clamoring fans.

One day, while Emory unloaded a dozen paintings from the pickup, Granny dragged herself into the studio looking tired and discouraged. "Viola, I tell you what, this here fame is wearing me down. I'm happy the gallery is finally making money, but I can't keep up with orders. We got to do something."

In a panic I said, "Don't give up, Granny! All artists have to suffer for their craft. You can't just stop giving the art world what it craves. Think of the gallery, think of your bank account."

With a tight little smile, Granny said, "Listen to you, Missy. Where's your talk of the muse now? So I'm working day and night for the bank account? When do I get to take a break and enjoy some of these earnings? Raise the prices, and then maybe they'll leave me alone." With a sigh, she shook her head and shuffled back to Emory's truck. We never got around to fixing our cup of herbal tea. I reached for the tranquillizers, for the first time in weeks.

Word spread to Capital City, and eventually crept like an advancing fungus to cultural centers across the country. Granny Frick was hailed as the new Grandma Moses, and the prices of her creations increased tenfold. The art world was vying with itself to analyze the small town phenomenon, and Purple Palette became the happening place to visit. Articles about the exhibit appeared in the New York Chimes, Peephole, and Charade. A TV network flew Granny to New York to be interviewed by Wynn Frey, the popular and powerful talk show host. He pretended to know something about art, but he was unprepared for the likes of Granny Frick. Afterward, the show went into reruns for two weeks.

The new Frick style was dubbed Nouveau Naïf, credited with restoring an appreciation of the essence of things. Of course, I was given an occasional nod as the perceptive mentor who had discovered the hidden talent in Rock Bottom.

I found my new-found fame and fortune at odds with my artistic integrity. Was I the only one who perceived the reality of the situation? Was I the only person who saw the paintings for the dreadful eyesores that they were? Was it fair to nod and smile as I accepted thousands of dollars for *Tractor at Twilight* while all the *Cicadas in Ballet* collection was relegated to a storage room? Since I could not resolve these ethical conflicts, I suffered angst that could not be relieved by tranquillizers or herbal tea or magic brownies.

A solution to my problems came from an unlikely source, Granny herself. One morning, after yet another crazy weekend of receptions, interviews and sales, Emma Frick came to see me, alone. She had lost her fiery spirit, and slouched like a woman old and defeated. She held out a drawing to me and said, "Take a look at that." It was one of her usual grotesque renderings of trees, blue sky, and bright yellow sun. "This ain't my work. The art teacher invited me to Rock Bottom Elementary to talk to the kiddies about my paintings. One of the little girls gave me this. See, she signed it 'Debbie' across the bottom. All of a sudden, I saw my paintings for what they was: bad. You tried to tell me, but I wouldn't listen. Viola, I got to talk to you about something. Don't get me wrong; I appreciate all you done for me. Being an artist has made me famous and comfortable, but it ain't what I was meant to do with my life. I don't know how else to put it. We don't even take time out for a cup of yarbal tea anymore; all we do is count the money and work, work, work to sell more bad pictures to them poor fools out there. I want to quit, and give lots of the profits to the County for arts and music programs in the schools. Now, what do you think about that?"

I nearly jumped for joy. "Granny, give me a hug! Sit down, let me get you a cup of tea, and we'll compose a press release announcing your retirement. You will still profit from reproductions of your paintings and sales from the gift shop, but there will be no more pressure."

"Now you're talking!"

Granny's spirits were returning, in more ways than one.

We enjoyed a carefree afternoon of chit-chat. My headache dissolved, and when I served the tea, she spruced it up with an infusion from her Mason jar.

# 8

# GRANNY IN THE BIG APPLE

*by*

*Wynn Frey*

Occasionally in the talk show business, we get a guest who is an entertaining, unique character. That makes us look good because it draws the audience in, and they'll tune in to hear more of the same. I can usually manage the guests on my show, On The Carpet, by leading them into conversations they'd rather not address, or shutting them up when they want to talk about things that might make me look bad. If I like the guests, I'll give them longer time on camera; if they are uncontrollable, I'll cut to a commercial ahead of schedule and dismiss them while we're off the air. I needed a smashing interview that would propel me into prime time television. I was tired of fan mail from insomniacs, late shift janitors, and night guards.

We had one Hollywood loser who was convinced she was in communication with aliens from another planet. That would have been OK; the public loves a nut job like her. The problem was, she said I was one of the aliens living here to spy on Earthlings, and plot their overthrow and enslavement. Her cockamamie reasoning was that I had a device concealed under my hairpiece, and had the power to control anyone within six feet of me; that's why she insisted on sitting seven feet away from me on stage. You would have thought that interview would be the end of her career. No, her popularity took off like a space ship (excuse the reference), while my hate mail increased by 1000%. The studio was picketed by hundreds of strange people wearing green grease paint, Spock ears, or antennae made out of aluminum foil. They carried signs saying, "Down with the Alien Spy" and "Talk Show Traitor". We went into reruns for two weeks while the furor died down. Before returning to the air I had to agree to appear minus the hairpiece in future shows to allay fears that I was controlling guests.

There are some guests that every talk show host dreads: those that won't talk. Questions are answered with a "Yes" or "No", leaving the guy behind the desk scraping grooves in the furniture with his fingernails. Worse yet, once we had a famous Hollywood has-been who spent the interview time flirting with his current boyfriend standing in the wings. I couldn't compete with that.

Our network, Nadir Broadcasting System, scheduled the famous artist Emma Frick to appear on my show, and we flew her to New York first class on Pinewood Airlines. They have since cancelled their sponsorship of On The Carpet, but our lawyers persuaded them to drop the lawsuit. NBS spared no expense on Ms. Frick for two days of sightseeing in the Big Apple. She had a limousine tour, lunch at Lardi's and a personal tour of the Empire State Building, the United Nations and, most importantly for an artist, the Museum of Modern Art. We had her all softened up for an interview that was going to raise our standing in the polls.

I do not meet with guests before the show; we want to give the interview an air of freshness and spontaneity, so we meet for the first time when they make the long walk from the green room to my desk. The afternoon of taping, I heard a commotion coming from the area where guests are prepped and made up. I sent word to call my office with a report. It seems that Luigi, the hairdresser, was having a meltdown.

"The artist lady," he sobbed, "she not want to let me style her hair."

"Just do it, Luigi. Nobody asked her; we always spruce up the guests. She's from some place called Rock Bottom, for crying out loud. You'd think she'd *want* a makeover."

"You don't understand, Mr. Frey. This lady, she's different. She hit me with tote bag when I try to do something with the hair, and she threaten to call Sheriff."

"Okay, Luigi, calm down. If the broad doesn't want to look nice on national television, that's her problem. Just let it go."

The wardrobe department ran into similar resistance from the featured guest; she refused to wear anything but her own clothes. Wardrobe said to brace myself for her appearance. I figured that artists are renowned for their eccentricity, and she would surely not look any worse than some of our previous guests. There was the budding ingénue – and I do mean budding – who walked on stage in a skin tight see-through silky sheath, but no underwear. One musician of note looked so scruffy that security wouldn't let him onto the set, and he was held up for twenty minutes while we sorted out the mess. Never underestimate the strange taste of television watchers. Our viewing numbers shot up after each of those wardrobe disasters, so who knew how Ms. Frick would affect us?

At the 7:00 p.m. taping of the Frick interview, we had to set Ms. Frick straight about the timing of the broadcast. Someone had to convince her that she would truly be seen late that night, just as she had told her friends in Rock Bottom, and they still had time to catch a long nap before the show came on TV. We started off with my less-than-brilliant monologue, then had a guest who was the national champion breath-holder. Oh, boy. This show was sliding downhill rapidly.

The band struck up a fanfare and drum roll, and I announced our featured guest, the renowned artist from Rock Bottom, and former Mayor, Emma Frick.

The audience rose to give Ms. Frick a standing ovation, and she strode onto the stage in a gingham skirt, tweed box jacket, and high-top tennis shoes with crew socks. She was carrying a tote bag that had seen better days. When the hubbub died down, Ms. Frick smiled and waved to the audience which responded with another round of applause, then she turned to me and shook hands. She had a grip like a man. Ms. Frick kept craning her neck at the set.

"This here studio's not as big as it looks on TV, is it?"

Laughter from the audience.

"No, TV creates illusions, Ms. Frick, and sets do look larger from home. Do you watch On the Carpet?"

"Nope, sonny. My mama taught me to use furniture like a civil person."

"This show, Ms. Frick, is called On The Carpet. Have you ever watched it?"

"Ain't seen it but once, when I found out you folks was going to have me here. Nearly midnight is too late for a body to be awake. Some of us needs our beauty sleep." This, with a sassy grin directed at the audience. She knew how to play them, the clever old biddy!

Switching subjects, I asked her to tell us what she thought about The Big Apple.

"Which kind would that be, Mr. Frey? Golden or Red Delicious?"

"I mean New York City. It's referred to as the Big Apple."

"I sure don't know why they do that. In two days I ain't seen no apple trees in the whole durn city, 'less you got some in that big park in the middle. Looks like a good spot to bag some squirrels."

When the laughter died down, I said, "Ms. Frick…"

"Oh, you can call me Emma, just like everybody on TV shows calls each other by their Christian name."

"Emma, tell us about your plane trip to New York. I understand that was the first time you've flown."

"Well, Wynn, it was a big thrill to fly so fast and high over the earth, but them airplanes is uncomfortable and confining. A body can't get up and walk around without permission, and has to stay strapped in like a criminal. The nice young man who kept bringing us things was a nuisance, if you want to know the truth, and the alcohol he served wasn't near as potent as the liquid refreshment my boy Radcliffe makes. He kept trying to make me stay in my seat, even when I needed to use the john. I told him to go ahead and chuck me out of the plane 'cause I didn't want to have no accident right there in the aisle."

"Too much information, Emma!" More laughter from the audience. This was going well. "What did you think of the Empire State Building? Have you ever seen anything that impressive in Rock Bottom?"

"That building took my breath away, it was so tall - for a building, that is. Buzzard's Beak Point back home in Cornrow County is at least twice as tall, and if you're not careful you can slip off the edge. That happens every once in a while, when someone ain't careful or if they're climbing drunk. One thing you won't find on Buzzard's Beak Point is thieves. An ornery cuss tried to steal out of my tote bag right there on top of the Empire State Building! Can you believe that?"

While the audience laughed, I feigned surprise. "No! You don't mean it. Who would do such a thing? Did they take anything out of your bag?"

"Yep. Scroungy little fella that needed a bath real bad had his arm in my bag up to his elbow. He pulled out a strip of venison jerky I was planning to nibble on later. 'What do you think you're doing, you varmint?' I asked him. He said, 'Going fishing,' while he pulled his arm out slowly. I swung the tote around and whacked him good and hard aside of his head. The critter even reported me to the security fella, who told him to take a flying leap. Don't know how he could of done that, because there's high fences all around the walk outside."

"So, did you get robbed at the United Nations, too?"

"No, not robbed, just confused. New York folks is hard to understand because they got odd accents and short tempers so they don't like to repeat theirselves. There must have been people from every country on earth in that U.N. They was all gabbing in their own languages, and when they spoke American they was hard to understand, even harder than New Yorkers. The best part was seeing so many different colors of folks, all talking together and getting along like old friends. That's better than fighting, ain't it?"

This drew applause from the audience, and Emma Frick looked surprised but pleased.

"Just have to say, Mr. Frey, New York is a fine town, one of the best in the world, I imagine, and it pains me to see some of the poor folks on the streets here, and the terrible condition of the buildings some have to live in. The rich folks live in better places than I've ever seen, but the street people tear at my heart; even the worst trailer park in Cornrow County looks better. Surely a city this great could take care of its own!"

The applause was thunderous.

After a short ad break, we resumed. "Now, Emma, tell us about your meteoric rise in the art world. What is the inspiration for your paintings? What school is your favorite, and who is your favorite artist?"

"My favorite school, the one I went to, is the only one we have in Rock Bottom. God's green earth is my inspiration: the trees, the blue sky and bright sun; children and cows and tractors. All the things we see every day and may not remember to be thankful for. My favorite artist is Viola Haze, who taught me how to paint, and who sips tea with me when we need a pick-me-up."

Here we showed some of Ms. Frick's paintings on video. Privately, I thought they were horrible, but I pretended to know something about art, and praised them.

The audience played the same game, and clapped politely when the slide show was over.

It was time for another commercial, so we went off camera for a few minutes. Ms. Frick asked for a cup of tea, which we provided, then said it needed a little something. She produced a small Mason jar from her bottomless tote bag and perked the tea up, we're not sure with what. She fidgeted during the ad break, and started complaining.

"You know, Wynn, this is why so many folks like me don't watch television. Them ad folks is using up our time telling us half-truths, and want us to spend money on stuff we don't need and ain't good for us." She didn't know that in the middle of her soliloquy the show went back on air, and her words were heard by millions of viewers nationwide.

The loud affirmation from the audience didn't win me any friends with the producer or director, but I thought, wait until they see the ratings shoot up; then they'll give me a raise.

I managed to shut Ms. Frick up when she realized we were back on the air.

Now I was ready to pull out the stops, and turn the interview into my famous On the Carpet grilling. Too much "nice" gets boring, and isn't good for ratings. "Emma, you said you don't watch this program, or much else. Just what do you watch on TV?" I thought she'd say, soap operas and pork belly futures.

"Don't watch much TV anytime, Wynn. Been too busy painting, taking care of my garden, going to Bingo, secret shopping for TallMart, and serving on the School Board. Do like to watch news once a day to find out what's going on in the world, and for fun I like to watch bull-riding."

"You, Emma Frick? Bull-riding? What do you like about that sport?"

"Those nice young fellas are pretty brave to take on them ornery critters, Wynn. The poor things get all throwed and battered and stepped on, and they keep coming back for more. Also, their cute tight jeans make a body's heart beat faster!"

When the hooting and laughter from the studio audience subsided, I asked, "Isn't there something else you do that you haven't told us about, Emma?" Now it was nasty time.

"I ain't mentioned my age, if that's what you mean."

I closed in for the kill, "No, Emma, I'm talking about your family. Don't you have three sons who can best be described as 'worthless buzzards,' to quote their Maw? One is a bootlegger..."

"Just a minute there, Mr. Frey! Radcliffe is a bona fide businessman..."

"...one is in jail more than he's out..."

"...that ain't true! Duke has run up against a string of bad luck, is all..."

"... and the third one is a petty crook, dumber than a doornail."

Here I paused before coming in for the kill. "You have some secrets of your own, don't you, Bonnie? Tell us about your days in Harbor City, where the audiences knew you as Bonnie Butz."

Ms. Frick, to my surprise, kept her cool. She gave me a look that shriveled my – well, part of my anatomy. My Grandma would have said she had the Evil Eye. I shuddered a little.

"Mr. Frey, folks in Rock Bottom got troubles same as people here in New York City. Only difference is, we're kind to each other and don't rub their faces in the dirt in public, specially not in front of the whole country on TV."

The audience had become deathly quiet, and I hoped that was a sign they were fascinated by my personal brand of journalism. I began fantasizing about soaring ratings and promotion to prime time.

Ms. Frick continued, "Now, Mr. Wynn Frey, enough about me. Tell us something about yourself and your family, your pretty blonde wife."

Caught off guard by the guest turning the conversation in an unexpected direction, I stammered, "My wife is brunette, not blonde."

"You mean that lady you was kissing back there in the hallway was not Mrs. Frey? By the way, that there blonde hair is fake; look closer the next time you kiss her, and you'll probably see the dark roots."

I gestured frantically for a cut to commercials. "What do you think you're doing, woman? You're out of here, you hayseed moron." I had forgotten to muffle the mike, and the audience heard everything. All hell broke loose as the audience booed me and yelled for Ms. Frick to stay.

The producer standing nearby was loving it. He had been wanting to get some leverage against me, and now he would hold this over my head. "Mrs. Frick isn't going anywhere, Frey. She's a hit, and our percentages are going to go up after this show. Your biggest problem will be Mrs. Frey. If I were you, I'd order the most expensive diamond necklace I could find."

I hissed at Ms. Frick, "It seems the producer is on your side, but don't push it, lady. Let me put some spin on this and don't say a word, or we might go deeper into the subject of your sons and their illegal antics. Hmm? Do you want that splashed all over the scandal sheets from here to Rock Bottom?"

In a voice loud enough for the audience to hear all the way to the back, Emma said, "Of course I won't say nothing while you cover up, Mr. Frey. The threat to expose the bad luck my sons has had is enough to keep me in line."

When the commercial break ended, the band played their loudest to drown out the commotion from the audience, which was yelling at me and cheering for Ms. Frick at the same time. I played down the pre-break incident. "Welcome back to the exclusive On the Carpet interview with Ms. Emma Frick, eminent artist and woman of many talents. During the break we sorted out the misperception Ms. Frick had when she saw me kissing my cousin visiting from Chicago. Yes, Emma was right, Mitzi does lighten her hair. Bad, bad Mitzi! Right, Emma?"

Ms. Frick didn't answer or smile, just gave me a tight-lipped glare.

"Right, folks? Who here has naturally blonde hair?" Several of the audience clapped loudly, and most of them laughed nervously. That was enough to distract from the nastiness at hand. I started to go on with the interview, but Ms. Frick picked up her tote bag and walked off the set, with a final wave and kiss to the audience, which rose to their feet again and cheered her on her way. I tried to hold the studio viewers together for the rest of the show, but they were out of my control. The band played loudly and we signed off early.

The producer informed me we were going back into reruns for the next two weeks. At the end of that time, a decision would be made either to keep me on as host of On the Carpet, fire me, or give me the plum of prime time at last. The two weeks will be up in three more days. My whole future is hanging on Nadir Broadcasting System's decision, thanks to that hick woman from nowhere.

# 9

## GRANNY'S BEAU

*by*

*Emma Frick*

Wednesday is liver and onions day at the Senior Center, so naturally that's my social day. I visit with the other senior citizens, and I'm the youngster since I'm from five to forty years younger than most of them. Sometimes the Center has music or dancing by local groups, mostly children, who come for their schools or Scout Troops. We clap and give them lots of thanks and compliments, but, truth be known, I'd rather eat and visit in peace. That's the price we pay for being old folks getting a cheap meal and a day out.

The senior men have their pick of which lady to flatter, because there are mostly widows coming to the Center. The women who are looking to trap a nice widower can be spotted, easy. They get all prissied up, with thick smeary makeup, bangles and baubles bouncing, and hair done just that morning. They smile and laugh, even when nothing's funny, and look around sideways at the men to see if they're noticing. I can't do that; it just don't seem honest. Besides, Abner was the best husband in the world, and the only beau I could ever have.

I enjoy playing cards with the women – the ones who aren't playing silly flirty games with the fellas – or I just sit there knitting or reading. After the meal one Wednesday, I was minding my own business in the corner with a copy of Peephole magazine when a handsome gentleman come up to me. He was tall, and stood straight for his age, which I guess was near to mine. He had very thick hair that was snow white, like it had turned many years before its time.

"Good afternoon, Madame," he said in his nice deep voice, "may I join you?"

"Ain't no law against it," I answered. "You can set a spell, long as you behave yourself."

Laughing, he said, "Emma Frick, I do admire your directness. It is a breath of fresh air in this den of hypocrisy."

"How'd you know my name?" I squinted hard at him, trying to remember if we'd met before. Nope, couldn't recall ever being introduced to him.

"Your fame precedes you, dear lady." His voice was smooth as silk – or was it oil? "I have read about you in the Rock Bottom Rambler, but never before today have I had the honor to meet you." Here the varmint took my hand and kissed it! I yanked it away. "My name is Edmund X. Conner, but my friends call me Ed."

"Mr. Conner, what can I do for you?" I was leery of someone who come on so strong. "What did you read about me that was so darned interesting?"

He sat down and got serious. "Your fame and fortune as a nationally acclaimed artist; your bold leadership in the landfill scandal; your successful term of office as Mayor of Rock Bottom. I could go on and on. Unfortunately, some of your sons have made the Magistrate's Report, but let's not go there."

I answered, "You almost flattered me until you said something about my sons' bad luck. You're right, Mr. Conner. We won't go there."

"I would like to be friends with you and take you places where we can talk and have fun. Do you like dining at fine restaurants, visiting museums in Capital City, going to the opera?"

I answered, "I wouldn't know about that, because I ain't never done them things. You like to hunt, play Bingo, go to County Fairs, pickle cucumbers, and hoe the garden?"

Mr. Conner laughed, but he sounded a bit uneasy. My good friend Velma, a sensible lady without no pretending in her soul, was sick, and I'd wanted to visit her when my son's truck was out of the shop. "All right, Mr. Conner, I'll take you up on your offer. How'd you like to take me to see a sick friend, then we can eat at Betty's Kitchen afterwards?"

"That's a start, Emma." I never give him permission to call me by my first name. He must of seen me frown. "I'm sorry – Ms. Frick. Let's go now to visit your friend."

I told the man who drove the Senior Center van I'd not be riding home with him. He looked thankful. Mr. Conner – Ed, as I come to call him – drove a shiny expensive sporty car like nothing I ever rode in. The top was down, and it did feel good to have the wind blow my hair straight out. I was thinking, I could get used to this. "What do you do when it rains?" I asked.

"Simple. I put the top up." Then we both laughed. It was getting easier to be with him, and I made up my mind to take him as he was and not judge the man too much. Ed didn't pay much mind to the speed limit. He said he knew where the speed traps were, and where there weren't no cops patrolling. That made me a bit uneasy, not because I was afraid to go fast, but because I didn't like the idea of going against the law in such a brazen way. Have to admit, though, there was a bit of a thrill in doing something naughty. I laughed out loud at the thought of Jim Purgitt or his deputy chasing us down with lights flashing and siren going.

Ed put some awful screechy music on the radio, a Wagner opera, he called it. When I asked for Bucky Burke and the Bail-Jumpers he thought I was kidding and turned up the sound of the opera. Just before we reached Velma's apartment, Ed suddenly pulled into a shopping mall.

"I thought we'd take your sick friend some flowers," he said.

"That's mighty thoughty of you," I said. "I'll come in and pick them out."

"Oh, no, Emma, you wait in the car. I'll be right back." I guess he was trying to be kind and let me just set there like a lady and wait for him while that darned opera screeched. I turned the radio to a different station. He returned five minutes later with an arm-load of roses. "How's this for a bouquet?"

"Roses won't do, Edward. That's why I wanted to pick out the flowers. Velma's allergic to roses; she can't be in the same room with them. I could have told you, but you was bound to dash in by yourself."

"Mea culpa, I'll take them back and exchange them. And it's Edmund, not Edward. Ed will do." He looked kind of sour at the radio dial.

I said, "All right, Ed…and it's Emma, not Mea Culpa. I never heard of her."

So it seemed that we got off to a rocky start. Velma was doing poorly, but she liked the yellow daisies we brought her. Ed laid on sympathy with a shovel, then heaved a sigh of relief when we left. As I hugged her good-bye, Velma whispered, "Be careful of him, Emma. I don't trust him."

When we got back to the car he said, "Now, my dear, where is this ptomaine palace called Betty's Kitchen?" When did he think he got permission to call me "my dear"?

"Edmund, you sure ain't from around here, are you? Everybody in town knows where Betty's is. You can't miss it on the corner of Main Street and Possum Avenue. The cooking is plain and down home, but it never made nobody in Rock Bottom sick."

Ed got very quiet for a minute or two. "You're right, Emma," he said at last, "I'm from another town, but how fortunate I am that I found Rock Bottom! Had I not stumbled upon this gem, I never would have met you, and my life would be incomplete."

"Listen to you! You're what my Mama called a silver-tongued devil. You ever been married?"

Another moment of silence. "Yes, once or twice." Then he laughed, nervous-like. "Perhaps the third time will be the charm."

"You never said what you done for a living, Edmund."

"No, I didn't, did I? Let's just say I am independent, and have no need to punch another man's timecard."

I laughed and said, "My Mama used to call men without no jobs but with lots of cash and lady friends 'gigolos'. Ain't that funny?" Ed didn't laugh.

We pulled into the parking lot at Betty's Kitchen, and ours was the flashiest car there. Heads was turning as Ed came round to my side to open the door for me. It had been many a year since anyone done that. He made a body feel like a lady; I began to wish I still had a pair of them little white gloves and some patent leather Mary Jane shoes. He held open the door to Betty's Kitchen, and I noticed that it stuck a little and the screen had holes in it. We seated ourselves at the best table, near the jukebox. Betty give us some menus, and I was surprised to see stains and fly specks on them that I hadn't noticed before. Betty said, "Granny Frick, I ain't seen you here for a week or two. Our special today is the Reuben you like so much, and our dessert is coconut cream pie." To Ed she said, "Who's this? Don't think I've seen you in Rock Bottom before."

"Edmund X. Conner, Madame. I hope to see more of you as long as Emma will consent to accompany me."

"That so?" she said. "Well, you better treat Granny right, or you'll have me to answer to." I could swear I blushed. Betty was giving me a real odd look, but I tried not to look at her directly. Betty was a right hefty gal, broad-shouldered like a man. Not many folks would want her mad at them. I changed the subject by ordering the Reuben and pie. This was my favorite lunch ever, and Betty makes the best Reuben. Her coconut cream pie is about the closest thing to one of my own pies that I ever tasted. Ed ordered the same things I did, but he ate as if it smelled bad and was going to bite him. I found myself apologizing for the cooking, the restaurant, and the menu, and couldn't wait to get out of there and into the fancy red car. He paid the bill without leaving no tip, so when we was on our way out, I slipped some money onto the table. Betty saw me do it, and I hurried to catch up to Ed.

I asked Ed to leave me at my daughter Irma Jean's place in town. Something deep inside told me not to take Ed Conner to my house, at least not so soon. I rode the whole way without saying nothing. That didn't bother Ed, who talked about hisself and what we would do the next time we went out. "I do hope you'll wear a different color, Emma. Green is not becoming to you; maybe blue would be better."

I just said, "We'll talk at the Senior Center next Wednesday." He said he wouldn't be there on Wednesday because he hated liver and onions. Since Tuesday was baked chicken day, he'd be there then. That sounded too much like an order, and I thought, we'll just see about that, Mr. High and Mighty Conner. Liver and onions is good enough for the rest of us, why not you?

Next Tuesday come, and I was mopey. Edmund had not called me since we went to Betty's Kitchen together; I was missing the high-faluting thrill of driving around in an expensive, fast red car, and turning heads when he treated me like a lady. I felt there was a whole world out there I had missed out on when I married Abner, good man though he was. Abner was plain folk, and I never thought of him like that before Ed Conner squired me around town and showed off. Me and Abner had fun at the County Fair, shooting at the booths, and watching the pie judging contests. He always swelled with pride when I carried off first prize for my rhubarb pie, and I let him beat me at shooting so's he'd have something to brag about. With Ed, I knew it would always be different. I'd be apologizing for being me, and going places I didn't want to go, just to keep him from looking down his nose at me and my friends. Still, part of me really wanted to hear from him, and go to fancy places just to say I'd been there. I called the Senior Center van to pick me up at 11:30. I put on my fancy blue dress from Jeers and dusted my face with a little rouge and powder.

I tiptoed into the Senior Center, hoping no one would see me, but looking around for Ed. I spotted him kissing Carrie's hand; she is one of those who is looking for someone like him. I turned to leave, but some of the women saw me. "Emma, how nice to see you here on a Tuesday for a change! Did you come for the chicken, or for the Methodist Church Children's Choir?"

Carrie said, "I never seen you so gussied up, Miz Frick. Look at this, makeup and all! Maybe those rumors I heard is true, about you being seen around town on the arm of a fine gentleman."

I was blushing for sure, and Ed stood there with a little smile on his face. At last, he rescued me like the gentleman I hoped he was. "The rumors are true, dear ladies. Emma and I have been painting the town red. We have great plans for tonight, and next Saturday."

Pleased and embarrassed, I nodded and patted my hair, which I'd just had blued that morning. "Oh, yes, we're just the cat's meow, going to all these fine places. Which one are we doing tonight, Ed? I know you told me, but I must of forgot."

"Tonight, a poetry reading at the Frazzled Bean coffee house in Midville. There is a Philpott Philharmonic concert in Capital City on Saturday, to celebrate the opening of the new art exhibit at the von Snobbins Gallery. As an artist yourself, you will appreciate the vibrant cacophony of the twenty-first century compositions, both musical and visual."

I was tickled to hear the ladies ooh and aah, but gritted my teeth at the thought of sitting through poetry tonight. I ain't read poems since I read Mother Goose rhymes to my kids. An art show on Saturday could be fun, but I wasn't too sure about the music. I played along, though, and did my part to show the gals how classy we were. "That's right, Ed; tonight will be as exciting as a turkey shoot."

We rode to Midville mostly without saying nothing. Seemed I didn't have much to talk about that Ed would want to hear. The ride wasn't as fun as it was the first time, and I fretted because my hairdo was getting messed up. It was like he read my mind. "Really, Emma, must you dye your hair blue? A soft ash blonde rinse would be so much more flattering, and would take years off your appearance."

That steamed me. "So now you're a hairdresser, too? How I fix my hair is nobody's business but mine, Ed, and I'll thank you to stop telling me how to dress, where to eat, and what to do for fun." He acted real hurt that I spoke to him that way, and I felt bad.

Right away, I apologized for being so cranky. "You've been real nice to me, Ed. I'm sorry I spoilt the evening."

"I, too, am sorry that you have misconstrued my intentions, Emma. I just want you to put your best foot forward and become the best you can be. Together we can be a fantastic team."

"What kind of team? Bridge partners?"

He laughed, kind of nervous. "No, dear lady." Wished he wouldn't call me that! "I have an idea I've been wanting to run by you. I have the opportunity to invest in a new business that is guaranteed to take off like a rocket. If we go into this together, we will be wealthy beyond your wildest dreams."

I was confused. "How can I help you, Edmund? I ain't got no cash for no hare-brained idea like that. Ain't nothing in this world with such a guarantee on it. My wildest dreams have nothing to do with money, anyways."

"Emma! What about the fortune you made with your art? The profits are still rolling in from that."

"Did your homework, didn't you, Mr. Conner? Well, for your information, I don't have much left from that art fortune. I gave it to the schools for their art and music programs, and helped my art teacher to add onto her gallery."

Ed got real quiet. This time I wasn't sorry for what I said, so I was quiet, too. I was thinking about my Abner, and how he would never have bossed me around the way Ed Conner done. Even though Abner was a country boy through and through, he had more manners and kindness in him than this slippery fella with all his uppity airs. We was pulling up to the Frazzled Bean Café, and I had some plans Ed didn't know about. Inside was so dark we had to hold onto walls to get to a table. There was a tiny stage up front, with a stool and a mike, lit by a blue light. Somebody was plucking a guitar, but it was just noises, not music.

Ed ordered some coffee he called ex-presso, and started to order some for me. I got up the gumption to tell the waiter to bring me a yarbal tea instead. Folks was smoking, and it weren't all tobacco; I smelled that smoke before, when the good-for-nothing bunch my son Duke used to hang around with showed up at my house one night higher than kites.

A scruffy little fella that needed a shave real bad stood on the stage and started to recite his poem. It didn't make no sense, but the other folks thought it was worth clapping for. It had something to do with poor folks and pitchforks. Then, a hungry-looking gal with long tangly hair went up and sat on the stool. "My poem is called *Veggie's Lament.*" She looked mournful for a while, then recited:

"Fruits and vegetables, living things.
Growing, sensing, feeling.
*Loving.*
Skinned alive, sliced and diced.
Thrown screaming silently into the pot so that cannibals, gorged on the flesh of their fellow sentient beings, can consummate their orgy with salads and soufflés."

The audience gasped and stood up clapping loudly, while the poet bowed and wiped tears from her face. I thought, "These folks is either nuts, or they been breathing too much of this smoke."

I excused myself and went to the ladies' room, where I did three things. First, I borrowed a woman's cell phone and called Irma Jean to come pick me up in Midville; when I told her to come to the Frazzled Bean Café she was pretty unhappy that Ed brought me there. Irma Jean said she had been doing some Doodling on the computer, and was going to make some phone calls before picking me up. Second, I washed the rouge off my face and smiled at myself in the mirror. Then, I took out a pencil and a wad of paper I had in my purse and wrote a few lines.

I went from the rest room to the stage, and sat down on the stool. The crowd had calmed down from their excitement over the thin gal's poem, and waited politely for me to have my say. "My poem," I said, "is called *Liver and Onions.*" I put on my specs and squinted at the wrinkled scrap of paper in the blue light.

"Liver and onions is better by far
than raw fish and caviar.
A Conning man will bring you strife,
but an honest one lights up your life.
Don't need to change the colors I wear,

or the way I fix my hair;
I'd rather be just plain old me
than a fancy phony s.o.b."

The crowd was real quiet at first, then they jumped up and clapped and whistled. When I found my way back to the table, Mr. Conner had left, as I hoped he would. Someone come into the café and said there was flashing lights outside, and some fella had been taken into custody for fraud and scams. I sipped the yarbal tea and smiled to myself as I waited for Irma Jean to come pick me up.

# 10

## GRANNY COMES CLEAN

*by*
*JoEllen Dyer*

I n every small town the information center is the beauty parlor, as everyone knows, and mine is no exception. My shop is called the Beehive, and every lady in Rock Bottom knows it's always buzzing with the latest gossip. Everybody knows everybody else in this here community, and they discover most of the town secrets while under a hair dryer. There's something soothing and relaxing about having someone else shampoo and set your hair, do your nails and give you a facial. A body gets comfortable and trusting, and will tell the most surprising things about theirself and each other.

The ladies of Rock Bottom have seen each other through marriages, divorces, affairs and family troubles. Naturally they take the gossip home to their families, and within a week or two everyone in the town knows the news before the Rock Bottom Rambler gets ahold of it. Most important, they know what color hair each other really have, and by unspoken agreement never mention that to the other ladies.

My name is JoEllen Dyer, and my job is to keep all the gals happy and beautiful. My sister Bobbie helps out three times a week when she's not having morning sickness, but she's not as sociable as me; I have a feel for giving the ladies what they want. Some who don't like each other much, like Granny Frick and Miz Hanks, I never schedule their appointments on the same morning. The ones who work the late shift at the plant like to sleep in, then come for late afternoon appointments. Some need to rush in as early as possible so they can get primped up before they go to work in the bank or office. This one wants a certain shade of red hair dye, and no other will do; that one wants only a shampoo and trim, and another one wants the works. We have one nice young man who comes to the Beehive; he likes it here because the boys at Earl's Barber Shop give him a hard time. He is very polite, always smells good, and loves to have his nails done, though I talked him out of the mauve nail polish. I juggle schedules and products to suit the taste of each of my customers. It's a talent and an art, you might say, and I take pride in my work. Joan, a deaf girl who recently graduated from high school, cleans the shop, launders the towels, and shampoos the customers before I style their hair. Everyone feels comfortable talking freely in front of Joan; I'll never tell them she can read lips. She just smiles and keeps on doing her job. I've learned a little sign language, and when the shop is empty I'll talk some with Joan, who really is a smart gal but kind of shy.

Every once in a while we get a newcomer to town, and naturally they learn real quick that the Beehive is the place to go for beautifying and for gossip. There is one other beauty parlor in Rock Bottom, but it does not have the loyal following that I have. Rumor has it that some of their customers' hair has been singed by overheated curling irons, and simple bleach jobs have come out green. One day we had a walk-in, Maude Bellows, who was new to town, and lucky for her we had a cancellation. She was about sixty years old and plump, with teased hair and too much makeup that settled into the creases on her face, but her clothes looked real expensive like they came from Jeers instead of the TallMart down the road in Panhandle county. I think she could have updated her look if she had given up on hair teasing, but I understand that a lady beyond a certain age may have trouble with thinning, and a sure way to give the hairdo some body is to tease and spray it, so I didn't say nothing to her about being a bit out of fashion.

Maude seemed to fit right in with the regulars, and even though a newcomer has to be around for a long time before the locals will accept her, she eased into the group as if she belonged here. It wasn't long before some of the ladies were copying her makeup style, demanding the same aquamarine eye shadow and black eyebrow pencil that Maude used.

Miz Bellows seemed specially friendly with one of my younger customers, a pretty little gal named Charlene. Although Charlene says she's lived in Rock Bottom for years, none of us remember seeing her before just lately, when she took up with that good-for-nothing Cliff Frick, Granny's son. Not like the other ladies, Charlene never says much about her personal life, just makes small talk about hair, nails and clothes. Funny how she seemed to bond with Maude, a woman old enough to be her grandmother. They would chat together quiet-like, giggling and whispering like school girls, like they were sharing secrets. When Charlene wasn't there, though, Maude was pleasant to everyone and fit right in.

One day a real peculiar thing happened. It was a Thursday, Granny Frick's new appointment day, and she came in at her usual time, about 10 in the morning. Bobbie and I had our hands full, with more ladies booked than usual. Our newest customer, Maude, was scheduled, and it was the first time she and Miz Frick had run into each other. Granny hung up her hat and umbrella and nodded around the shop to Charlene and the other customers there, but she only glanced at Miz Bellows without any reaction. Maude stared all wide-eyed at Miz Frick, then laughed that big laugh of hers.

"Bonnie! I can't believe my eyes! Is that really you?" exclaimed Miz Bellows.

Granny Frick froze, then collected herself and sat down slowly, ignoring Maude and reaching for the old copy of Peephole Magazine I keep on the table for my customers. I jumped in, sensing that there was some tension, and trying to keep things friendly.

"Miz Frick," I said, "you haven't met our newest customer yet, have you? This here's Maude Bellows, who moved to Rock Bottom a couple months ago from Springfield. Miz Bellows, meet Emma Frick, one of my oldest - I mean steadiest - customers, and one of Rock Bottom's most prominent citizens. She's even had her picture in the Rambler!"

Maude held out a chubby manicured hand to Miz Frick. "I think we've met, JoEllen, but I'd forgotten her name." Then, low under her breath, Miz Bellows said to Granny, "I'll always remember you as Bonnie Butz, Emma. We'll have to get together and talk about the good ol' days, just me and you...about when we were *friends* in Harbor City."

Well, you might have thought that Granny had seen a ghost. She gasped and flew out of the salon so quick she left her umbrella on the hook. Her hasty departure was not lost on the other customers, who nodded and buzzed at each other for an hour. When Granny bolted, Charlene excused herself and followed her out of the shop: "I'll be back in ten minutes, JoEllen. Just hold my spot for me, would you?" Maude played her cards close to her ample chest, though, and wouldn't tell us any more about her past with Emma Frick except to say that they both had different names then, and looks change with time, so it was no surprise that Granny had not recognized her. Charlene didn't come back that day.

Granny Frick stayed away from the Beehive for two or three weeks after running into Maude. When she finally called for an appointment, she asked to change her regular day to Fridays. "That way," she said, "I'll be all fixed up for the weekend." That made sense, so Friday it was, but I reminded Bobbie never to schedule Miz Bellows on the same morning as Granny Frick because I knew sparks would fly if they met again. Poor Granny looked a fright the next time I saw her. Her beautiful natural hair was dry and lifeless and the bluing was wearing off. She walked all bent and tired, and her eyes had no mischievous sparkle, so I knew something was up. It didn't take a genius to figure out that Maude Bellows had something to do with Granny Frick's mood, so I tried to act cheery.

Good morning, Miz Frick! You've been making yourself scarce, haven't you? Been sick? Everything OK? My, you do need some hair care today, don't you? You look like something the cat drug in."

Usually Granny would give me a funny answer when I talked to her like that, but today she just took it and said nothing, so I began to worry about her. Joan set Granny down at the sink and began shampooing her while I got my scissors and other stuff ready. "So, Miz Frick," I said, "what're we going to do today? You want the full treatment, bluing and all?"

With a sigh, Granny answered, "Don't really care, JoEllen. Just do whatever you want."

Now I knew the situation was serious. I never remembered Granny not taking charge of her own hair appointments and telling me exactly what she wanted. I needed to talk to Miz Frick.

Bobbie wasn't feeling well, and her customer had cancelled, so I gave her the rest of the day off. Bobbie sighed with relief and said, "Thank the Lord." I signed to Joan to pretend, as usual, that she couldn't understand the conversation, then sat down next to Granny and took her hand. "Miz Frick - Granny - I don't know what's bothering you, but my gut tells me it has something to do with the new customer, Maude Bellows. Am I right? Don't say nothing right off, if you don't feel comfortable."

Poor Miz Frick snuffled and reached for her hankie, shoulders shaking and wet hair dripping onto the towel. I signaled Joan to go into the back room. She could clean up the shampoo sink later. Sometimes you have to take time to comfort someone, specially a faithful customer like Granny Frick. We're like a family here at the Beehive, and in all of Rock Bottom.

Everything poured out of Granny, all in a flood. "JoEllen, there ain't no way to run from your past, and mine has caught up with me. I knew Lottie - you know her as Maude Bellows - many years ago when we was young, and down and out. Harbor City was a place where folks could get work doing things they'd just as soon their families didn't know about. There was sailors, dockworkers, and others not as respectable who would pay to see a pretty gal with nice legs dance. Lottie Lipps and me – my stage name was Bonnie Butz – danced and stripped at the same lowlife bar near the waterfront. You can see why I'm shamed to run into her here; now she'll tell the whole town what I used to do, and my family will be sorry I'm their Maw. All the folks who voted for me as Mayor of Rock Bottom will be sorry they ever had a stripper in office. And I won't be able to hold my head up anywhere in town."

I squeezed her hand, "Miz Frick, take ahold of yourself! There's not one person on earth, or at least in Rock Bottom, who hasn't done things they regret. Why, I'll bet even Joan has secrets! You never hurt nobody, or got arrested, did you?" Granny shook her dripping head. "You wasn't doing tricks, either?" At this, some of Granny's pepper returned, and she pulled herself up.

"I never sunk that low, JoEllen. I seen what a struggle Lottie had to raise her daughter; she tried real hard to hide from her what she did every night, and it was always tempting to give in and make some extra money. We both had some morals in spite of the way we made a living. When things got better for me I quit the stage and moved back to this area, where I met Abner. Lottie lasted a few years more in Harbor City; it was harder to get out of that life when you had a kid to support. I was luckier. Lottie's – Maude's – daughter was caught up in the same life and gave birth to a baby girl when she was still a teenager. Last time I was here, Charlene followed me out of the beauty salon and told me the rest of the story. She's Lottie's granddaughter! The raising of Charlene fell to Lottie because the mama was too caught up in the life she was leading."

Then, the flood of tears started again. I caught sight of Joan standing and watching from the doorway of the back room. I frowned and shook my head, and she went back to folding the towels. I gave Granny tissues and a pat. "Your past is safe with me, Miz Frick. No one is going to talk about it, leastwise Miz Bellows; she won't want it spread around about herself, either."

"You don't know the rest, JoEllen. Charlene and Radcliffe want to get engaged, and I've been against it. Charlene has a past, too, right here in Rock Bottom on the Fruit Tarts' stage. The last time I was here

Charlene followed me out of the shop and put it to me real blunt, that she and Radcliffe were going to get engaged, and I shouldn't stand in their way. Maude Bellows is her grandmother, so Charlene knows all about Harbor City. No wonder the girl followed in her grandmother's footsteps! Funny thing is, I really like Charlene. She's spunky and smart, and seems to care for Radcliffe, but I can't bring myself to give my blessing to a marriage between my son and a..a..."

"Dancer, Miz Frick? Like you were? Don't you think that's a little harsh? Miz Bellows is a real nice lady. A little gaudy, but real nice. She's become a part of the Rock Bottom community and is here to stay. I believe that Maude and her granddaughter will keep your secret – and theirs – so you don't have to worry anymore." With that, Granny calmed down a bit and took a deep breath.

She said, "With a good listener like you around, JoEllen, nobody needs a head doctor. You're right, I shouldn't worry about the rumors. Lord knows, I've had to put up with worse in my day, and never before gave a hoot what people thought. Yes, I do like Charlene, and think she will make a good wife for Radcliffe. He's seen her dance at the Fruit Tarts, so no surprises there. He ain't exactly an angel hisself, so maybe he'll straighten up for her sake. Before we got engaged, I told my Abner about Harbor City, and he never asked questions or held it against me. I always thought I was the luckiest woman alive."

"Now, Miz Frick," I said, "it's time to finish your hairdo and send you out of here with a smile on your face." I cut, blued and styled her hair just like nothing had happened, and she walked out of the shop with her usual determination to take on the world. I told Joan we would close early since there were no more appointments that day, but she hesitated like she had something to tell me.

"Okay, Joan, what's on your mind?" I asked.

Joan signed to me, "I saw Charlene talking to Maude Bellows while they were here, and I read their lips. Maude came to Rock Bottom to be with her granddaughter."

I said, "Well, I know that, Joan. Charlene told Granny Frick."

Joan then said something that rocked me back on my heels, and I knew it would be another challenge for Miz Frick: "Charlene is pregnant."

# GRANNY AT THE BEACH

*by*

*Emory Frick*

Once Maw and me went to the beach. She had won a pile of money playing Bingo at the Volunteer Fire Department and said she wanted to spend it on something she never done before. Since my truck was out of the shop and my driver's license wasn't suspended, I drove her. Lucky for me I had no job at the time, so I didn't have to explain nothing to a boss. The beach was a long way from Rock Bottom, and it took us two days to get there.

All the way there, Maw was as excited as a little kid. "Finally, Emory, I'm going to set eyes on the ocean! I've waited a lifetime to see the beach; this is going to be more fun than hunting."

I had to admit I was pretty excited, too. Seeing pretty gals in them skimpy little bathing suits was what I was waiting for. "Hey, Maw, if you're going to go in the water, you have to have a bathing suit. We can't just wear our underwear like we do in Hogwaller Creek in Rock Bottom."

"Don't worry, Emory, I already got me one through a catalogue. I knew that someday them pesky catalogues would come in handy. The suit's the same color as jeans, and has a little skirt to hide all the bulgy parts."

The trip seemed to take forever, but we didn't get lost even once. Maw took charge of the map, seeing as how I'd never read one before. The truck acted up a few times, but as soon as something fell out on the road with a clank, it seemed to run better. I wasn't inclined to look into what had fell out. We drove through states we had never been in, and couldn't hardly understand the folks because they all talked funny. The first night we camped out in a nice spot where there was running water and vending machines. I thought it was just fine, but Maw grumbled some and said she was looking forward to staying in a real motel at the beach, like real tourists do. Travel was costing us more than Maw expected, and I was afraid her money would run out. "Don't worry, Emory," she said, "if there's Bingo places on the Boardwalk I'll win us enough money to get us home."

Finally, the second morning out, we saw a sign for Undertow City – only 108 more miles to go. It still seemed a mighty long way to me, but we'd come this far and sure weren't going to turn back now. On the way we had to cross over a big old bridge, and Maw was riled to find out we had to pay money (they called it a toll) just to drive over the bridge. It took her ten minutes of arguing with the lady in the little shed to convince Maw that the toll was legal, and everybody has to pay it or they don't use the bridge. Turns out the bridge saved us over a hundred miles of driving time and lots of gas, so the toll made sense after all; that, plus the toll-taker's threat to call the state police if we didn't move on. Drivers behind us was honking and yelling some real unkind things at Maw, but she ignored them.

The land was really flat as we got close to the beach. It was strange to go so far and not drive up hills and around curves. It was hot, too, without no trees to shade the highway. Along the road some farmers had set up stands to sell fruit and vegetables, so naturally Maw had to stop and take a look at what they growed. She was pretty impressed with their watermelons, and bought one for our lunch. Maw said their tomatoes couldn't match hers for size or color, so she was happy. I picked up a package of home-made cookies to go with the watermelon, but Maw made me go back and pay for them.

When we got almost to the beach town the breeze began to pick up and cool things off, and we smelled something odd; now I know it was salt water. There was all kinds of signs advertising restaurants, motels and shops, and they all had either pretty gals, white birds or seashells on them. I was tuckered out from the two days of driving and just wanted to rest, but Maw was all charged up and wanting to have fun.

We headed for the beach and staked out a spot on the sand where I'd get some shut-eye while she went exploring. Our first sight of the ocean shocked both of us speechless. We never seen such a big patch of water! The waves was even bigger than we expected – they could knock a person off their feet - and they hit the sand with such a boom, you'd think it was the Fourth of July. They didn't stop, either, just kept coming and coming; it was enough to make us dizzy, the way the waves never let up. I was almost in a trance, trying to think how it was possible for water to act like that. Maw was running around, setting up the beach stuff she'd bought at Bullseye. As soon as the umbrella was up and the towels down on the sand, I laid down for a nap. The sound of waves banging on the sand made me just want to sleep. Maw took her big tote bag and headed down the beach.

A long time later I woke up with the feeling I was being watched. When I opened my eyes, I was staring into the face of a big old gray and white bird. It pecked at the towel I was laying on, and squawked. I was wondering if it was fit to eat, and regretting that Maw hadn't brought Ol' Betsy with her. I gave the bird a cracker and all his buddies flew over and started fighting, screaming and pecking the towel and my hair. I yelled and jumped up, and they took off. I heard some giggling, and some pretty gals laying on the sand next to me was whispering, so it wasn't just them birds I felt watching me. I was just about to introduce myself, when I saw Maw coming back from her walk on the sand.

Maw said she'd found some treasures, and I got my hopes up; I had heard about pirate's gold. I should've known Maw was kidding. She dumped out the stuff from her bag, and she had quite a haul. I never seen real seashells before, and was right impressed with them; they was all different pretty colors and sizes. Maw held one up to my ear and I pulled back because I didn't want any little critter popping out to bite me.

"Hold still, Emory; don't you want to hear the ocean?"

"Maw, that don't make no sense; I can hear the ocean loud and clear already, so why would I want to hear it through one of them shells?"

"Good point, Sonny. They're pretty to look at, anyways; think I'll decorate my garden with them when we get home, and put some on my coffee table. Get your lazy bones up off the sand and let's go in the water."

There was little tents on the beach, and you could change into your bathing suit in one of them; problem was, they wanted money to let you use them. That didn't sound right. It wasn't no matter to me if people saw me change clothes on the beach, so I went ahead and did it. I had borrowed my brother Cliff's trunks, which was in fashion: bright red with Dale Earnhardt, Jr.'s face on the butt. Maw was more reluctant to share her naked self with the public, so she complained and handed over the money so's she could have privacy. A whistle started blowing while I was taking my clothes off, and one of them lifeguard fellas came over with an unhappy look on his face.

"What do you think you're doing?" he asked in that funny accent.

"Just changing into my bathing trunks. Can't afford them tents. What are you doing?"

"Getting ready to have you arrested, yahoo," he said, real mean-like.

"What on earth for? I'm just minding my own business," I said. "Indecent exposure."

"I don't know how indecent it is," I answered, grinning, "I don't hear any complaints from these pretty gals here." At that, the two young ladies lying on the blanket near my towel laughed out loud and said to the lifeguard, "Let it go, Charlie. We haven't enjoyed anything else we've seen today as much as this. You should be so indecent!" They kept on laughing, but I didn't see what in thunder was so funny. Charlie the Lifeguard turned red and stomped away, and the pretty gals acted real friendly to me. They invited me to sit on the sand with them, and give me some of their drinks. The blonde said her name was Jackie, and the redheaded gal was Vickie. They said my name like they was out of breath - Emmorrry – and ran their fingers through my hair. We was having a good time, and they was whispering some real naughty stuff in my ear when Maw came out of the clothes-changing tent in her bathing suit. I didn't even know she was standing there until she whapped me with her tote bag.

"I can't even go out of sight for ten minutes before you find bad company! Look at these here hussies with everything hanging out; they might as well be naked."

I answered, real sassy-like, "They would've been if you'd been a couple minutes later." Then me and the gals laughed so hard we couldn't stop. I was already feeling woozy from whatever they gave me to drink. It must have been powerful stuff, because I never got a buzz that quickly before. Maw hit me again with the bag and told me to get over onto my own towel, and told the ladies to go cover theirselves. Jackie leaned over and said, real low, they'd be in that spot at 9 p.m. if I wanted to party. I wondered whose birthday it was, and thought I should at least pick up a card. My gut told me I'd best not tell Maw I was going to a birthday party after bedtime, so I kept it to myself.

Maw looked right nice in her bathing suit, considering how old she was, way over fifty. She was on her way to the edge of the water, and I hurried to keep her from getting knocked over by them waves. The closer we got, the higher and scarier the waves looked, and the towel back up on the sand was beginning to seem like a safer place to be. Maw, though, was marching right into the water – surf, they called it – like she was a fish going back home. We could feel the ground shake when the waves hit the beach, and they made a noise like thunder. For such a warm day, the water sure was cold; my teeth were chattering, but Maw didn't seem to notice. The wind and waves just seemed to excite her. We splashed around a little, and got knocked down a few times by extra big waves; it was surprising how strong water could be, and I felt like I learned a few things I'd never thought about before. Hogwaller Creek was never going to impress me again, unless it was up over its banks in one of them floods we get every ten years or so. It could wash away trailers and cows, and leave old tires in the tops of trees, but the waves at the beach could do that on a good day when it wasn't even storming.

Standing up to waves is hard work, and we got tired. We decided to dry out and get something to eat. This time I kept my pants on instead of trying to change in the open and maybe getting Charlie the Lifeguard pissed off. Problem is, no one told me how it feels when sand gets up inside wet bathing trunks; believe me, you don't want to find out. Another surprise was how fast the sun can toast a person. Maw and me both got red because we didn't put on enough of that greasy stuff that she bought at Bullseye. We'd know better tomorrow. The boardwalk was full of nice stands where we could pick up hot dogs, cotton candy and such, but the food was more expensive than we expected it to be.

Maw said, "Emory, one stand's got corn dogs, and you know how I like them, but another one farther down the boardwalk's got hot dogs and fries for the same price; let's go there."

I was sorry to see Maw pass up corn dogs; I gave her five dollars from my chewing tobacco stash just so's she could eat in style. We washed it down with lemonade – which tasted a lot like dishwater, not nearly as good as Maw's hand-squeezed lemonade – and treated ourselves to some famous candy called salt water taffy. That was the best stuff I had ever put into my mouth, except for Maw's venison jerky! I couldn't get enough of every flavor they had, and when Maw wasn't looking I grabbed another handful out of a bin.

By sunset we were ready to settle in. We pulled into a motel, the Funky Flamingo, that was painted a real ugly shade of pink. Maw said it was called salmon, and they probably chose that awful color because it sounded like a fish. The folks who ran the place was snooty and acted like we wasn't good enough to stay there, until Maw pulled out her wad of Bingo money. They give us a room around back, ground floor, and we unloaded the large drawstring Lefty bags we had packed our things in. The motel was classy, decorated inside with paintings of big pink birds on the wall and lamps made out of plastic driftwood. Maw and me each had a huge bed big enough for half our family. There was TV and a telephone, and an extra sink to wash up while someone else was using the john. We left a window open and could hear the banging of the waves in the distance; the sound made us real sleepy, but I had to stay awake. Maw didn't know I had made plans to join the gals at the birthday party, and I figured what she didn't know couldn't hurt me. As soon as Maw was snoring I turned down the lights and TV sound, and snuck out to find Jackie and Vickie. The guilt I felt at sneaking out made my stomach hurt and heave.

I could hear loud noises coming from the beach, and thought, "Oh, gee, the party has started and I'm late." I pulled some taffy out of my pocket, planning to give it to the birthday person. The party was bigger than I expected. Jackie and Vickie were there, and so were about a dozen of their friends.

I said, "Hey, there! Who's the party gal?"

Half a dozen ladies said, "I am, Emory!"

I said, "Whoa! I ain't got enough candy to go around for all of you." For some reason, this cracked them up and I thought they'd never stop laughing.

Somebody shouted, "Where's your cash, Bubba? Partying ain't free, yahoo."

I thought that remark was real insulting, and I told them so. "My name ain't Bubba, and I ain't no yahoo. Where I come from, if we're invited to a party and bring a gift, we don't have to pay to get in; that's not neighborly."

Jackie and Vickie came over to me, one on each side, and put their hands in my pockets. Like I told them, I didn't have no money on me.

"What's this?" asked Vickie as she pulled out my wad of Cuckoo Chew.

"That there's my tobacco chaw, lady. I'll thank you to put it back. And now I'm going back to the motel; this ain't the kind of party I thought it would be."

Just then some of the fellas grabbed me and drug me to the water. "Want to meet some sharks, Bubba? Here you go!" With that, they tried to toss me into the cold water. I got really scared and twisted around, fighting to stay on land and not get eaten by no fish in them dark waves. I was no match for four men, though, and they drug me to the water's edge and threw me screaming into the ocean. I bounced out almost as soon as I landed and high-tailed it for the motel while they hooted and hollered behind me. I was soaked through, cold, scared and embarrassed. As luck would have it, Maw was sitting up on her bed waiting for me.

"Don't say nothing, Maw. I'm not in the mood."

"You look cold, Sonny. Go take a nice hot shower; you'll feel better." Maw was looking at me sharp, with a kind of twinkle in her eyes. "Maybe later on you'll feel like talking about things."

"Don't think I will, Maw, except to say I think I growed up a little bit tonight." I thought, worst of all, my Cuckoo Chew got soaked.

"Get ready for some pain, Emory."

"Thought we wasn't gonna talk about things right now."

"No, I mean the trots. Them corn dogs must of been bad, and I've been having trouble for a while."

Maw was right; the rest of the night we took turns in the john, and come morning we was almost too tired to move. We didn't want to start the day watching waves coming and going, coming and going, and getting dizzier and sicker. We decided to spend a few hours on the boardwalk, then relax on the beach later in the afternoon. The thought of even looking at corn dogs turned our stomachs.

Maw said, "Emory, later today I want to buy souvenirs for the family, and pretty pink plastic birds for my garden. I want to send postcards to everybody in Rock Bottom, and eat in style, at a table in a sit-down restaurant like elegant folks.

"But, Maw, that's going to cost a lot of money, more than we got."

"Right you are, Sonny. Sooo…it's time to find us a Bingo game and make a killing."

We asked around where the Bingo game was. Folks looked at us like we was speaking a foreign language, and shook their heads. Finally, a nice little old fella in a jogging suit took the time to tell us about casinos. Bingo ain't their game, but there's lots of others to play, he said. He suggested Maw try some blackjack, and after looking at me, said probably slots would be my speed. Somehow I suspected that there was not a real compliment. Up ahead we saw lots of blinking colored lights, spelling out "Lucky Buck Casino", so we headed for it.

Inside was like some awful nightmares I've had. It was so smoky I choked, and Maw didn't even want to light up. The sounds were loud and confusing, like a carnival, only lots louder. There were voices, music, coins clinking, roulette wheels whirring, buzzers, bells, whistles, and shrieks from gamblers who won a pile of money or groans from losers who had just missed their chance at thousands. My first feeling was, I'm scared and want to bolt for home, but Maw just looked the way she does when she sets her mind to something: her lips go into a tight line, and she charges right in.

"Don't fret, Emory. These games are here to be won, and that's what we're going to do." With that, she gave me a handkerchief full of quarters and told me to set at one of the slot machines and keep feeding coins into it until she had won enough money for us to go shopping. After I lost all the quarters, which didn't take too long, I wandered around to see what I could see. There was some pretty gals with very tight clothes and short skirts walking around helping the gamblers, giving them change, selling cigarettes and so forth. Two of them looked awful familiar, then I realized they was Jackie and Vickie; I almost didn't recognize them, dressed as they were with a few more clothes on than when they was at the beach. I wanted to buy some more chewing tobacco but Jackie laughed at me and said, "You gotta be kidding. Go away, hayseed."

I tried to talk with Vickie, but she told me to buzz off. The folks in these parts sure wasn't into hospitality. I found Maw sitting at a table with some other gamblers while a man dealt a deck of cards to them a few at a time. "This here's blackjack," she whispered to me as she picked up a bunch of chips, "It's easy to win if you can remember which cards has been played." Maw seemed to be doing real well without my help; she had a big pile of chips in front of her, and every hand the pile grew bigger. She gave me another bunch of quarters, and I headed for the slots again.

It didn't take long to lose all them quarters; no wonder the slot machines is called one-armed bandits. This time I found Maw hauling in her chips again. She had a little smile on her face, but the fella dealing blackjack looked pretty upset.

"Doing right well at blackjack, Emory. How's two thousand sound?"

"Two thousand quarters? Maw, it'd take me most of the day to lose that many in the slot machines!"

"Two thousand dollars, Sonny! Think I'll stay here a little while longer. Whooee! We're going to shop in style, Emory!"

Sure enough, Maw couldn't be stopped. Her chips was piling up again, and pretty soon two big mean-looking men who didn't look like they had ever laughed in their lives stood behind Maw's chair, one on each side. A man with greasy hair, who seemed to be their boss, said to Maw in his funny accent, "Okay, sister, you're done. Out. No card counters allowed at the blackjack table."

"You ain't Maw's brother, and you ain't my uncle," I argued with him, but Maw hushed me up. "It's alright, Emory, we've had our run. I think I'd best try something different, that won't interfere with other folks' chances at winning. I'll get me some more quarters and try that machine you been playing." I showed Maw which slot I'd been feeding quarters to, and she set to work. After only three tries, bells started ringing, lights flashing and sirens going off. "What in thunder is that?" she cried. One of the pretty gals in a tiny skirt said, "You just won the jackpot, Ma'am! This must be your lucky day. This young man sat here all afternoon without winning, so I guess he warmed the machine up for you." Maw collected a heap of money, more than we'd ever seen at one time in our whole lives. She took some of it in silver dollars, which I'd never laid eyes on before. On our way out of the casino, Maw stopped at one of the dollar slots and just for fun put one coin in it. What do you know, it happened again! Same old bells and lights went off, and Maw got another pile of cash. This time the folks in charge weren't as friendly, and we decided to skedaddle when the two mean-looking fellas headed our way.

"Well, Emory, ten thousand will get us the best pink flamingos in Undertow City, and a fine dinner in a real restaurant with menus and cloth napkins."

"Maw, how do you know about them things? I never heard you talk about menus and cloth napkins before."

"Emory, our lives change. I done lots of things you don't know about, and it's best we leave it at that. Just like we done last night." With that, Maw smiled and pinched my cheek like she done when I was little.

The next couple of hours was spent in shops on the boardwalk. Maw had a great time buying souvenirs for the whole family; nothing made her happier than spending money on us and her friends. She always said money was just a tool, a way to do something you want to do or get something that will make you or someone else happy. Guess that's why she never has no extra in the bank. Being lucky at Bingo gets her over a hump lots of times. She bought bright shirts with parrots on them for Cliff, Duke and Hunter, and a colorful flowered skirt and an orange floppy hat to match for Irma Jean. She bought Laurie and Caltech a lamp made out of real seashells and a neon green plastic salad bowl set to put aside for their wedding. She got Charlene and Cliff strings of red lights shaped like crabs and ashtrays made out of big thick shells. For all the folks in her life Maw bought the best of everything in the shops: bobbing hula dancer dolls, long dangly earrings, sunglasses with starfish on them, and big straw purses with spangles and shells all over. Most exciting, Maw finally got her pink flamingos for her garden. They had wings that would whirl when the wind blew. She laughed and said the crows would probably keel over when they saw them big birds flapping, and would leave her garden alone. I thought she wasn't going to buy me nothing, but I didn't mind because she had treated me to this great time at the beach. Truth is, I wasn't crazy about wearing no shirt with parrots on it, so I kept my mouth shut. Just before we left the last store, though, Maw handed me a five-pound box of salt water taffy! That made my day, but she wouldn't let me open it until after dinner.

For the rest of the afternoon we just laid around on the beach and took it easy. The clouds was the prettiest I had ever seen, and the squawking of the birds – gulls, someone called them – and the booming of the waves sounded like a kind of music. It was going to be hard to leave tomorrow morning.

By evening the effects of the bad corn dogs had wore off and we was hungry, so we found a classy restaurant called Chez Chuck that had signs saying, No Bare Feet; Proper Attire Only. I didn't know exactly what attire was, but it seemed to mean my truck wouldn't be allowed in because the tires was bald and patched. The waiter set us down in the back of the restaurant behind some palm plants. Guess he knew we wanted privacy while we ate. There was things on the menu I never heard of, but Maw said anything we ate there would be good. I let Maw order for me because she seemed to know what she was doing.

The waiter brought a cart of hors-something-or-other. I couldn't believe they'd even use a word like that in such a nice place, but the food was good even though I had no idea what them little girly things was; guess that's why they called them hors. We ordered oysters, and that was a mistake. I had heard that oysters was supposed to make a man more like a man, so I was willing to try, but they was raw! I'm not real squeamish, but the oysters was too much. When I squeezed lemon juice on them, one flinched, and I'd had it; Maw ate hers and mine, too. The bread was right good, and I stuffed my pockets with some to gnaw on in the truck the next day.

When the waiter asked what vegetables I wanted, he acted snooty when I said my favorites, grits and black eyed peas, so I ended up with mixed vegetables that was so undercooked they was crunchy. He didn't know I saw him laughing with his buddies behind Maw's back, looking at us and sneering. I didn't say nothing because I didn't want to hurt her feelings, or get her so riled up she'd whap him with her tote bag.

Maw said, "What else do you want to eat, Emory? How about celebrating big with a whole lobster?"

"Don't know, Maw. It ain't gonna be still alive, is it? I don't think I can tolerate another critter quivering as I eat it."

"Nope, Sonny, I promise the lobster will be deader'n a door nail."

You never saw such an ugly dinner in your life! This big ol' dead thing that looked like a giant red bug in a horror movie was setting on my dinner plate with its eyes looking right at me. It had claws as big as hammers and a hard shell all over it so that you had to work to get the meat out. The waiter gave me tools for the job and a bib to catch the mess I'd make, but I say any food that causes you that much sweat had better look prettier than that. Lobster kind of grows on you, though, and after a while I got used to yanking the meat out and dipping it in melted butter. After dinner Maw ordered dessert, but I was saving myself for the salt water taffy she bought me. They brought her some apple pie, and Maw was real happy to find that it wasn't one bit as good as hers. We was so full we had trouble walking out of the restaurant. Because Maw had won so much in the casino, she was in a generous mood and gave the snooty waiter a big tip; the ornery cuss changed his tune and was falling all over hisself to thank her as we waddled out.

We both slept sound that night, though I did have strange dreams about big red bugs with bibs on. The next morning Maw was smiling to herself, like she had a secret. "This has been a good two days, Emory. I loved seeing the ocean, but I'll be glad to get back to Cornrow County. How about you?"

"Me, too, Maw. I seen things I never thought I'd see, but home is the best place. I just hope the truck will make it in one piece."

"There's one more place I want to go on our way home, Emory. When we get about five miles west of Undertow City, slow down."

I thought maybe Maw wanted to go into another souvenir shop, but that wasn't what she had in mind. "Pull in here, Sonny."

I asked, "Are you sure? This here's a used car lot."

"You got that right, Emory," Maw said with that little I've-got-a-secret smile. "You're always driving me around in this wreck, and I think it's high time we got you a new used truck."

I nearly crashed into one of the shiny cars on the lot, I was so surprised. "Maw, do you mean it?"

"You should know by now, I never say nothing I don't mean. You're good about driving me all over creation, and this trip is one of the best things we ever did together. I'd say that's a good reason for a nice surprise."

So that's how I got my new truck. I picked out a classy bright red one without no dents or rust, and it had good tires that should last a while and a working radio with all its buttons. The seats had no rips or stains, and our feet didn't stick to the floor. Maw paid $3,000 for it with her winnings, and I felt bad about that because that's about six times more than I ever paid for a truck. She said that still left her with several thousand dollars, which she was going to save for special family occasions.

I had a sneaking suspicion that didn't mean bailing out Duke again. It might mean something about additions to the family, but I'm keeping my mouth shut until it all comes out.

# 12

## GRANNY AND
## THE GAMMA RAYS

*by*

*Deputy Sheriff Billy Buster*

### INCIDENT REPORT # 130429

**Name of Complainant: Emma R. Frick**
**DOB Dec. 16, 19.. [Complainant refused to divulge year of birth]**
                                              **SSN: 999-00-7643**
**Address: County Road 7, Box 58, Rock Bottom, Cornrow County**
**Phone: 555-000-1846 email: n/a**
**Date of Complaint: July 31, 2011**          **Time: 8 a.m.**

**Nature of Complaint: Trespass by person or persons unknown; possible theft; sightings of unusual green lights.**
**Officer Responding: Deputy Billy Buster**

T he Department responded to a call at 8 a.m. from Ms. Emma Frick, residing on Thistleburr Lane, off County Road 7, five miles north of Rock Bottom. When the Sheriff's Deputy arrived, the complainant was agitated, and handling an ancient shotgun which she indicated was loaded. I persuaded her to put the weapon away and tell me why she had called the Sheriff's Office. While her accusations were wild, the clues were intriguing. She showed me her vegetable garden and there were unidentifiable prints between the rows of plants, and vegetables and whole plants were missing. The complainant described seeing green lights descending the hill on the other side of the valley on the nights when the thefts and vandalism of her garden occurred. Mrs. Frick expressed her suspicion that the green lights were gamma rays, and that the odd impressions in the dirt were the footprints of aliens from outer space. A local TV news show had reported sightings of UFOs in Cornrow County, and the complainant is convinced the inhabitants of alien craft are responsible for raiding her garden.

Because of the evidence of damage and theft, I agreed to return at night the next time Mrs. Frick sees the green lights on the opposite hill, and I took pictures of the strange footprints for analysis by the Department.

**LAB REPORT, reference Incident # 130429:** The prints photographed at the scene of complaint, August 1, 2011, on Thistleburr Lane, County Road 7, are sunk in the soil to a depth of ½", indicating that they were caused by a heavy person walking on the garden soil. The prints showed a cross-hatched pattern, with a solid line around them as if some sort of footgear had been worn, possibly attached to ordinary shoes. Some imprints were consistently deeper than others, suggesting either that there were two individuals trespassing in the garden, one heavier, or that one individual walked with a limp. No further conclusions can be drawn until more evidence is found.

## INCIDENT REPORT # 130671

**Name of Complainant: Emma R. Frick**
**DOB Dec. 16, 19.. [Complainant refused to divulge birth year]**
**SSN: 999-00-7643**
**Address: County Road 7, Box 58, Rock Bottom, Cornrow County**
**Phone: 555-000-1846 email: n/a**
**Date of Complaint: August 5, 2011            Time: 2:36 a.m.**
**Nature of Complaint: Sightings of green lights moving down the hill across the valley from complainant's residence and garden.**
**Officer Responding: Deputy Billy Buster**

The Department responded to a call at 2:36 a.m. from Ms. Emma Frick, residing on Thistleburr Lane, off County Road 7, five miles north of Rock Bottom. When the Sheriff's Deputy arrived, Mrs. Frick was agitated but unarmed, and she pointed out the lights descending the hill opposite her property. She said it was the alien from a UFO. I observed small green lights moving down the hill, disappearing behind trees and reappearing in clearings. I instructed Mrs. Frick to remain in the house, and then waited in concealment for the lights to come closer. Eventually a figure emerged from the direction of the hill; there were two green lights for eyes, and it shuffled along with a limp. I waited until it entered the garden, and when I heard the sound of plants being torn out I stepped forward with flashlight and gun raised and ordered the suspect to put his hands up. The person snarled and cussed, sounding more like a man than an alien from a UFO. When he turned around, I saw he was wearing a night-vision binocular head-set, which I ordered him to remove. He was carrying a sack in which he had stuffed some vegetables and plants from Ms. Frick's garden, and on his feet were strapped a pair of old tennis rackets with their handles removed.

Ms. Frick came out of her residence and recognized the suspect. Identifying him as Shadrach "Crazy" Egan, she said, "Shadrach! What the blazes are you doing in my garden?" The suspect replied, "Hey, Miz Frick. I got chickens and eggs, but the soil up on my hill ain't fit to grow nothing. I like some salad and vegetables from time to time, and you got plenty."

Ms. Frick said, "Why the heck didn't you ask? You didn't have to scare me half to death with them green-light goggles; I thought you was an alien from a UFO. What's the footgear for?"

"I didn't want to leave any footprints. I've had enough troubles with the law, and folks around here don't like me."

I asked Ms. Frick if she wanted to press charges against Mr. "Crazy" Egan, and she declined. "No sense in punishing a man 'cause he's hungry. Tell you what, Shadrach, I'll make a deal with you. You and me'll trade every week: chicken and eggs in exchange for vegetables and salad stuff, how's that? No more sneaking down the hill at night and scaring a body silly."

I issued a verbal warning to "Crazy" Egan about trespassing and helping himself to garden produce, but when I left the premises at 3:30 a.m. the complainant and Mr. Egan were on good neighborly terms.

Submitted by Cornrow County Deputy Sheriff Billy Buster, town of Rock Bottom.
August 6, 2011.

# 13

## THE BEAR AND OL' BETSY

*by*

*Shadrach "Crazy" Egan*

My neighbor, Miz Emma Frick, lives across the valley from my hill. She's the only one in Rock Bottom who gives me the time of day, but I don't care none – they're all no-count except Miz Frick, and I'm glad they pretty much leave me alone. Emma is a good lady, though, and has a heart of gold even though she can give a body a look like the evil eye if they done something she takes exception to.

One night I heard a ruckus in my henhouse. From the sounds coming from that direction, I feared something big was after my chickens, and figured I'd best be staying inside until it went away. Caution is better than courage, in my opinion, specially when it comes to defending something as dumb as a chicken. The light of day showed a pitiful sight. The coop was all in pieces, and most of the birds was dead or missing. In the dirt was the biggest bear paw prints I had ever seen. Scared as I was, I knew something had to be done about this critter, or all of us in these parts were going to have trouble. The only one I cared about, though, was Emma Frick, who'd always done right by me so I had to do right by her.

Grabbing my Grandpappy's muzzle-loader, I tromped down the hill and across the valley.

Miz Frick saw me coming and met me at her garden fence. "Early, ain't you, Shadrach? We usually trade on Thursday."

She exchanges garden stuff with me for a chicken and some eggs every week, and she's the only one in Rock Bottom who calls me by my Christian name instead of "Crazy".

"We got trouble, Emma, and I come to you for a warning and to help. Big ol' sumbitch bear done got after my chickens and pretty much wiped them out. I couldn't face him alone last night, so thought maybe you an' me an' Ol' Betsy could take him on together. You're the next nearest property, so I reckon he's headed this way soon."

"Think we need more hands, Shadrach. The two of us can't do much damage to a bear like you describe. Let me call my boys." With that, Emma phoned her useless sons one by one. Cliff was out of town on "business", Duke was temporarily visiting the Sheriff, and Emory was laid up with his "third case of mumps". "Worthless buzzards," said Emma. "Guess it's you and me, Shadrach, unless we call Jim Purgitt to give us a hand."

"No, ma'am, I've had enough doings with the Sheriff and his Deputies; don't want them doing us no favors. We'll handle this ourselfs. Them offspring of yours don't measure up, do they? Sometimes kids is hard to wean."

We had to come up with a plan. There was no guarantee the bear would show up that night; it might be a week or more before his raid. Bears is crafty and smart, and can outwit you on any given night. Emma agreed to let me camp out on her porch where I could hear the bear if it started tearing up the yard. I had my night-vision binoculars with me. I had got them a couple of years ago, rather not say how or where. I prepped my muzzle-loader so it would be ready when I needed it. Truth is, I was scared as I've ever been in my life, but Emma was almost excited to see the huge bear for herself.

The skinny moon was mostly hid by clouds, which was good for my night-vision glasses. I waited and slept on the porch for four nights, but nothing happened. On the fifth night the sky clouded over and it started to rain about 1 a.m., just the kind of night that would bring out a bear. Sure enough, through the sound of raindrops I heard some snorting and woofing, so I turned on my night-vision binoculars and took aim with my gun. There was a huge shape in the garden, flinging plants around and eating everything in sight. I tapped on the window and Miz Frick turned on the lights and brought Ol' Betsy outside. I shone the flashlight on the bear, and it stopped what it was doing and turned to face us. He was about the size of a tool shed, but there was something odd about the way he moved and looked at us, like he was having some trouble seeing. He sat on his haunches and waited for something to happen.

Emma cocked Ol' Betsy and took aim, then lowered the shotgun and said, "Shadrach, look at that bear's eyes. He ain't got but one, and that's why he's acting funny; he can't see too well."

I said, "You're right! He must have been a force to reckon with when he was in his prime, but now he's just a scavenger raiding henhouses and gardens because he can't hunt no more. Almost feel sorry for the poor sumbitch." I took a good long look at that old critter, and couldn't help but see myself in him. Poor old broken down animal, forced by circumstances to live like an outlaw; people hating him just because he raided farms to stay alive. We wasn't going to be around much longer anyways, neither of us.

Miz Frick must of been thinking them kind of thoughts, too, because she hesitated. The bear plumped down on the dirt and snuffled around in the vegetables he'd torn up. She looked the old bear in the eye and gave him her famous evil eye look, but I thought I saw her lip tremble a little. "You varmint," she said, "get the heck out of my garden and go get your vittles somewhere else;

and you leave Shadrach's chicken coop alone, too, you hear? Next time around, we won't be so forgiving."

With that, we readied our guns together, aimed, and both shot at once over the bear's head. The explosion was enough to scare the critter out of its skin, and it roared and took off running down the valley. If we had had any sense, we would have done him in that night, but we just couldn't bring ourselfs to do any more damage to such a mighty fine animal.

For a few weeks after that night, Granny heard reports that a huge bear had been visiting farms in Panhandle County. Folks never knew what happened to Gramps, as the bear was called, but eventually the raids stopped and no signs of him were ever seen again. Some of us would like to think that the poor ol' critter went peacefully to his own Henhouse in the Sky.

# 14

## BIRD WATCHING IN ROCK BOTTOM

*by*
*Mavis Oxford*

My name is Mavis Oxford, President of Rock Bottom's bird watching club. I am writing this memoir about Emma Frick as a favor to Hunter Tydings, who is collecting stories of her exploits to put in a Chronicle. Hunter and I have been friends since grade school, and I have always considered him to be one of the more sensitive members of Rock Bottom society. The same can't be said of that woman, and I rue the day she came to me and asked to join the Tweeters. I sensed trouble when she marched up to me on the street and announced she intended to take up a hobby, and bird watching was her choice. I had misgivings that were rooted in gossip about the Fricks, and in personal disappointment. Hunter Tydings had fallen in love with Granny Frick's daughter, and while I don't blame him for that, I still feel the sting of rejection.

"How...interesting, Miz Frick" I stammered. "Granny's" reputation had preceded her, and I could not picture her having the patience and gentleness to observe our feathered darlings without causing disruption. I had no idea. "What made you pick birding over, say, bowling or crocheting?"

"Hard to say, Missy," she replied. "Tried bowling once, and just didn't get any excitement over knocking down them little wooden things. Crocheting don't get a body out in the fresh air for exercise like the doctor says I need. Watching birds sounds like what I do anyways, so I thought I'd give it a try. OK if I bring Betsy?"

"By all means," I replied, "your friend is welcome to join us."

Our next trek was scheduled for the following Saturday, starting at 6 a.m. Since it was early March, still cold at dawn, and with unsettled weather threatening to give us sleet, I hoped Granny would stay home where it was warm and dry. Our brave little band of five Tweeters set out a little late and navigated the obstacle course of mud and potholes in Greta's old van to the appointed spot, arriving at 6:20 a.m.

"Where in thunder have you folks been?" There was Granny, sitting on the running board of an ancient rusted pickup and smoking. Her attire was, I must admit, completely correct for bird watching: sensible walking shoes, comfortable shapeless raincoat that had seen decades of hard use, slouchy waterproof hat over her unruly blue-gray hair, and a formidable set of binoculars. Maybe she might fit right in with our group, or so I thought.

When Granny stood up to join us, the driver's side door of the derelict pickup opened and a hairy, wild-eyed creature emerged. Several of us gasped and involuntarily stepped back. It appeared to be somewhat human because it was wearing clothes and oversized boots, but no one had groomed it in weeks, from the look of its unkempt hair and scruffy facial growth. It displayed a wide tooth-deficient grin and said, "Hey there! Brought my Maw 'cause she don't drive. Don't mind me. I'll just set here and sleep in the truck while you all go around chasing birds."

Granny said, "Duke, where's your manners? You didn't introduce yourself. This here's my youngest son, Duke. He's a good boy, but can sometimes be a worthless buzzard. I'm lucky he's out on bail this week, otherwise I couldn't have made it today."

"Oh, thank God!" muttered Greta Hawkins, imposing and severe, the most dedicated member of the Tweeters.

"A buzzard is a bird, too," guffawed Duke, while spitting a blob of tobacco juice, "so I got something in common with you all." That tickled his funny bone, so he kept on giggling and whooping until long after we started on our hike. We could hear him carrying on for a good ten minutes.

Grinding out her cigarette in the mud, Granny said, "That Duke is a trip. He always did have a sense of humor; that and his good looks will get him a girl some day. You married, Miz Oxford?"

"Uh, no, ma'am, but I'm engaged," I lied. We were familiar with the infamous Frick clan through police reports and other evidence of nefarious deeds as reported in the Rock Bottom Rambler, but coming face to face with one of them was shocking. Changing the subject, I said, "Miz Frick, I'd like to introduce you to the rest of the Tweeters: Jay Boyd, Greta Hawkins, Corva Peck, and Robin Meeks."

"You can all call me Granny. Everybody does." She gave a sharp cackle, "Sonny, Robin sure is a peculiar name for a fella. Your folks should have been ashamed of theirselves."

"Miz Frick!" I exclaimed, "That was inappropriate. Robin is a fine name dating back many centuries, and Mr. Meeks is an upstanding member of our club."

"Too bad he doesn't know his birds," sniped Greta Hawkins. Her birding Life List was much longer than anyone else's in the club, and she never let us forget it. Jay had suggested that some of the sightings on her list may even have been faked, an ethical disgrace in the world of birding. I never doubted Greta's list because she and her husband used to travel widely, never living long in the same place; she had many opportunities to spot unusual birds that we in Rock Bottom have never seen.

In his usual gentle fashion, Robin smiled sweetly and replied, "It's all right, Mavis. Granny is right; I've had to deal with my name all my life, but have come to terms with it among friends." He adjusted his thick, round owlish glasses, drew his tweed floppy hat down over his ears, and pressed on through muck and mire, a true birder to the core. Wistfully, Robin added, "The Meeks part, though, is hard to live down."

"Weren't you going to bring your friend, Betsy?" I asked Miz Frick.

She gave a tight little smile and answered enigmatically, "Ol' Betsy is always with me, Miz Oxford." I did not know what she meant by that, but was not inclined to pursue it. I should have.

Corva's black spiky hair made her look like an angry raven. She was on edge because we always made her leave her cigarettes behind when we went birding. She sniffed and glared at Granny Frick. "What are you doing here, anyway, you old bat? Do you even know the difference between a Cooper's hawk and a Sharp-shin?"

Tight-lipped Greta added, "Hear, hear!"

Jay stepped into the fray. "Cut it out, ladies! We are *bird watchers*, not common brawlers. Calm down and *watch for birds*, okay?"

"Oh, good heavens!" exclaimed Greta. "I was so flustered by the ... appearance ... of our new member that I utterly forgot to bring my binoculars out of the van! Go ahead and I'll catch up with you." With that, Greta strode off down the muddy path toward the parking spot and we plodded along.

Jay said, "By the way, Granny, my Pa used to go hunting with your husband, Abner."

"That right? Maybe you and me can bag a buck together next fall." Granny brightened up, now that she had found common ground with one of the members. I must give her credit for having spunk and stamina. She charged on through thickets and mud at a punishing pace, leaving us younger Tweeters struggling to keep up. When we came to a sheltered glade, everyone grew hushed and watchful. We took up our stations, facing in different directions to spot whatever might be hiding in the trees and brush.

The sound of feet squishing through the marshy ground proved to be Greta Hawkins returning with her binoculars. Her jacket was full of burrs and her new hiking shoes were even muddier than ours. A bit out of breath, she gasped. "That creature is sleeping in his truck, and his snoring is so loud that every bird within a half mile will disappear."

"Then you're in luck, Missy," said Granny, with a steely look, "we're about twice as far as that here, and there's all kinds of birds in them reeds."

Granny was right. A marsh is a wonderful place to observe wildlife, especially the feathered kind. Even when we didn't spot the birds, their unique twittering gave them away. The small marsh was bordered by mixed deciduous woods and some brushy meadow, so it presented a varied environment for many species. With a flurry of excited whispers, we identified the bird calls. "That was a black-throated blue warbler!" "I hear a veery." "Was that a red-winged blackbird?" "No," with a sniff, "that was a common grackle." A sudden squawk took us by surprise: "Awwwk! Buck, buck, buck!"

"What on earth..." exclaimed Greta, "could that have been the elusive green heron?"

"Naw," said Granny, hooting and slapping her knee, "that there's a chicken."

To our surprise and chagrin, Granny was right. Coming from the meadow and strutting across the path in front of us were three plump domestic fowl.

Old Shadrach Egan lives just up there on Turkey Hill," said Granny, "and his chickens is always running loose. They're looking good, just about ready for the pot!"

Corva fumed and shook her head. Greta glared and muttered under her breath. Robin ducked his head and pretended not to hear.

We used our bird calls, argued about what we heard and saw, and had our usual jolly time in spite of Emma Frick's presence. Robin took photos with his digital camera, Jay made notes, and I recorded bird calls for later study. We all observed nest-building activities and referred to our handy field guides. Occasionally when she got bored, Granny wandered off to follow the chickens.

Growing tired from our intensive bird watching, we took a snack break of trail mix and power bars. Granny, however, reached into the depths of her raincoat pockets, brought out some disgusting brown twisty stuff, and started gnawing on chunks of it.

Greta Hawkins just had to ask, "What on earth are you eating, Miz Frick?"

Granny beamed and answered, "Made it myself, Gretel. Venison jerky. Last fall, this big old buck wandered into my yard, and I took care of him. Got stacks of jerky put up in my shed. I got some extra here; want some?" Even tough Greta shrank in horror at the offer. "Next time I'll bring jerky for all you folks." We couldn't wait.

Since the pale murky sun was beginning to sink and a cold wind had picked up, Robin suggested we head back to the van. I was thinking that the walk had turned out to be more successful than I had dared hope it would; things certainly could have been worse. Granny trotted ahead of us, occasionally ducking off the trail and poking around in the brush. On the way back we had our best sighting of the day, which had us all a-twitter: a barred owl hunting while it was still light. Tolerant of our presence, he hooted and swooped and gave us quite a thrilling display. As we compared notes Robin remarked that Granny Frick had been separated from us for some time, to which Corva snapped, "Count your blessings." Just then a terrible explosion startled all of us. I screamed, Robin dropped onto the ground, Corva swore, and Jay frowned. The boom was followed immediately by a second ear-shattering noise. The barred owl disappeared, and the other birds we had been watching shrieked and took off in several directions. Robin cowered under a bush, and even Corva whimpered.

"I know what that was," said Jay, still scowling, "I know a shotgun when I hear it. It came from over this way." Jay started to lead us in the direction of the shots.

"This is a wildlife preserve," I said. "Who would have the audacity to shoot here?"

"I can think of one person," said Corva, "that disgusting redneck who drove Miz Frick here. Duke."

"Not just Duke; Granny, too. Look." With that, Jay stepped into a small clearing where Granny stood grinning and holding up two trophies.

"Good shooting, by golly!" crowed Granny. She cradled a shotgun in the crook of her arm, and two dead birds dangled from her hands: a limp chicken and – heaven forbid – a male ruffed grouse! "When I shot the chicken, this here grouse was flushed from cover and I got him with the second barrel. Hah! Ain't lost it yet! This here's Ol' Betsy." She nodded at the ancient shotgun as she slipped it back under her ample raincoat. "We been together for a long time, and she's pulled me through some tight spots."

They tell me I fainted, dropped like a stone where I stood. When I came to, Corva was attending to Robin who was retching in the bushes, and Jay was arguing with Miz Frick.

"You stupid woman," Jay bellowed, "you can't just go into a county park with a weapon and shoot the wildlife off-season. Don't go anywhere, I'm going to call the Sheriff."

Granny spoke up confidently. "Won't do any good to call the Sheriff," she said smugly. "Weren't no county law broken here today and I can prove it."

"What are you talking about?" asked Corva while patting Robin on the back.

"Thing is, we're not in the park right now. See that marker on the tree over there? We left the park, the wildlife refuge and the county when we passed that spot. Sheriff Purgitt ain't got jurisdiction here, and he won't do no favors for that Sheriff in the next county by turning me in for the grouse."

"What about Crazy Egan?" asked Robin, who had recovered enough to stand up. "He owned that chicken."

"You folks don't know much. Shadrach and I have a deal. This ground here just next to the park belongs to Mr. Egan. Sometimes we swap, fair and square, but sometimes it's more fun to play the game. He sneaks into my garden at night when no one's around and helps himself to vegetables; in return, I take a chicken now and then. We both pretend we don't know who's doing what; it makes the chasing and catching more exciting. Go ahead and ask him if you don't believe me."

We began the hike back to the car, Granny trudging on ahead. When we neared the parking space, she called, "Dinner tonight, Duke! Me and Ol' Betsy done it again."

Corva, eager to get her cigarettes out of her purse, was first to reach the van.

"What have you done with my purse, you moron?" screamed Corva. "I left it here in the van, and it's missing!"

Duke replied, "Ma'm, you're crazier'n old Mr. Egan. I ain't took no purse; my Maw would whup me if I did that to one of her bird chasing friends."

"My whole life is in that purse! Give it back to me now, or I'll call your parole officer."

"Duke, Miz Peck, hush up!" Granny snapped. "No need to get all riled up. Duke wouldn't never do that with me in shouting distance; had to be someone else took the purse."

Just then Greta, who had dashed to the van and was rummaging through the back of it, raised her voice. "Miz Frick, I demand to know what your son has done with our purses! He is the only one who had the opportunity to rob us."

"Wait," I said, "I am going to call the Sheriff." With that, I climbed into the van to retrieve my purse and the cell phone in it, but to my shock, my purse was also missing.

Jay Boyd came to the rescue. "My phone's in my pocket, so I'll call the Sheriff." With a triumphant look at Granny, he added, "This time we are back in Cornrow County, and Sheriff Purgitt has jurisdiction."

The late-afternoon sun was behind clouds and the damp air began to chill us, so we got into the van to keep warm. Greta turned the van so that it blocked Duke's pickup truck and prevented him from driving off with our purses. While we sat and waited for the law to arrive, Granny and Duke were prowling about the grounds, looking at the dirt and poking in the bushes. Corva and Greta fumed and called the Fricks a few censored names.

While Granny squinted at the soft ground in the parking area, Duke went crashing into the thicket next to the stream. A few minutes later he emerged with a jack-o-lantern grin and three dripping wet purses in his hand. "Found 'em!" he yelled. "They was in the water near the bank, under some bushy branches. You ladies is lucky!" He spat a generous gob of tobacco juice in our direction.

"Lucky, indeed!" said Greta, "You surely don't think we believe that you 'found' them?"

"Not so fast, Missy," said Granny. "All of you bird watching folks listen to me. You track birds and know which ones they are by the clues you pick up. You study their nests, you listen to their songs, you see a woodpecker hole or owl poop. Well, I've been tracking all my life, and I can prove that this here theft was not done by my Duke."

Timidly, Robin spoke up. "We should at least hear her explanation, don't you agree?"

We grudgingly decided to let her talk until the Sheriff arrived; at least that would keep the two of them occupied.

Granny began, "Duke wasn't the only one here in the parking area. Ms. Hawkins came back to the van, and she's the one who took them purses. She even took her own to throw suspicion on Duke." With that, a chorus of angry protests interrupted her. Robin again spoke up on Granny's behalf. "Let her finish," he said, with something that sounded like authority.

Granny continued, "How did Miz Hawkins turn on her van? She had put her car keys in her pocket instead of leaving them in her purse. Go ahead and look in the other two purses; I bet you'll find keys, cell phones and everything else in them except the money, but her purse is probably mostly empty."

Jay volunteered to check out the purses, and announced that Granny was right: my purse and Corva's had most of our things in them - except the money - but Greta's was empty.

"If you check Gretel's jacket pockets, you'll find all the stuff that should've been in her purse. There's more," said Granny. "I spotted the prints of them expensive new shoes of hers in the dirt, leading from the van to the stream, and when Duke went in that direction to find the purses, he came back covered in burrs. Did you see them burrs anywhere else on our walk today? Only on Miz Hawkins when she came back from the van with her binoculars."

Our embarrassment at having misjudged Duke was surpassed by our sorrow at learning that one of our own Tweeters was a thief. I asked, "Why, Greta? We are your friends, and we trusted you." She glared darkly at me and turned her head away.

Sheriff Jim Purgitt arrived with a deputy; any incident involving the Frick clan always called for extra precautions. With a smile and a tip of his hat, Jim said, "Afternoon, Mavis. Those birds been giving you trouble again?" The sheriff had been in the same class with Hunter Tydings and myself and for years was sweet on me; but I always had eyes for Hunter so our relationship remained just friendly. I thought to myself that he did look dashing in his sheriff's uniform, and his smile and wink made me feel good.

"Oh, it's not the birds, it's much worse than that." We explained the situation and Greta even admitted, somewhat defiantly, that she had taken the purses and money.

The Sheriff was impressed that the crime had been solved even before his arrival. "You again, Miz Frick? Seems every time I get a call lately, you're already on the scene."

Granny grinned and said she had to admit that was true. "Have some jerky, young fella?"

"Thanks, Granny, I sure will. Your homemade venison jerky is the best in Rock Bottom!" With that, Sheriff Purgitt escorted poor Greta to his car. Before driving off, he turned to me and asked quietly, "How've you been, Mavis? I don't see you around much any more. You and that Tydings fella still dating?"

"I'm doing fine, Jim. I work at the Rock Bottom Rambler as a proofreader, and most of my spare time is devoted to the Tweeters. Hunter is engaged to Irma Jean Beck; you know - Granny Frick's daughter. He and I have not dated for a long time."

"Well, that is very interesting, Mavis. I owe him a thanks for that." Honestly, I was blushing by the time he loaded Greta into his car. Before they drove off, Granny hustled up to him and pulled him aside. There was much whispering and bobbing of heads, then Granny and Sheriff Purgitt both spoke to Greta. When Jim drove away, Greta Hawkins was in tears and Granny returned to us with a satisfied little smile.

"He's going to drive Miz Hawkins home so you can use the van and return it to her later. I borrowed her keys."

"What just happened, Miz Frick?" I asked. "Is he letting that thief go without arresting her?"

"Mavis, your friend Greta has got some problems. She says she and her husband moved around a lot because she kept getting into trouble stealing things. She promised Jim Purgitt that if no charges were made against her, she would go to one of them head doctors and get herself straightened out. Now don't that make more sense than jailing that poor unhappy soul? She's too embarrassed to join you bird chasers the next few weeks, but I think she wouldn't mind some kind words from you folks once in a while. The Sheriff has got the money she took from you, and he'll see you all get it back. Jim asked about you, Mavis," Granny grinned conspiratorially, "and I told him you were engaged, so don't worry 'bout him bothering you no more. Not even Duke has a chance with an engaged gal."

Granny Frick got serious. "Miz Oxford, you bird watching folks coming here again next week?" I nodded woodenly. "Well, Missy, I got to tell you I ain't going to be here no more. It just ain't my cup of tea. You've all misjudged me and Duke from the start. I even tried to get on your good side by talking Jim Purgitt into letting Miz Hawkins off. You folks and me don't mix, that's plain. Too bad for you, Mavis; you might've had a good catch in Duke."

We solemnly bade the Fricks goodbye, and drove home silently, almost in shock. True to the birders' tradition of forging ahead no matter what the obstacles, we eventually agreed to meet again, but at a different venue. No one had the heart to return to the scene of the crime, and those of us who were not yet vegetarians converted soon after.

# 15

## GRANNY SEES THE LIGHT

### by
### *Emma Frick*

T his here is a witness to something that most people will probably not believe, but it is the honest truth. I died and came back again, and dare anybody to say it didn't happen just like I say it did. It all started when I was working in my garden and overdid it a bit digging, lifting and hauling. There ain't never a son around to help you when you need it – worthless buzzards – so I was doing it myself. Next thing I knew, I was laying back against a tree stump, feeling real faint and weak, and trying to breathe. Irma Jean showed up at just the right time, and called the Rescue Squad. She gave me a swig of Abner's brandy, which I keep handy for emergencies or for visits from important people.

The nice fellas from the Rock Bottom VFD hurried me in an ambulance to the hospital over in Panhandle County, but I don't recall the trip; too bad, because I always wanted to ride in one of them things, with lights flashing and sirens going. A bunch of folks in white started working on me, but my memory is kind of fuzzy about what they did; here's what I do remember.

I began to feel real good all of a sudden, and was floating in the air over a bed where a handsome woman was being poked and prodded. A nurse and a doctor kept looking in each other's eyes, kind of flirty, and I reached down and yanked her hair. She stopped fussing with the medical stuff and looked around, real surprised, like, "who pulled my hair?"

I tried to say, "Mind what you're doing, girlie, that lady on the table needs your help. You can play doctor with the young fella later." The words didn't come out so's anybody could hear them, but they must have gotten into her head.

I soon realized it was me on that bed; I tried to tell the doctor folks not to worry, I was feeling fine now and they could all stop what they was doing, but they was so busy they didn't pay any attention to me. I heard sobbing out in the hall, and there was poor Irma Jean, crying her eyes out. I floated to her and said, "Now, don't cry, honey. I'm too mean to die; everything's going to be just fine."

She stopped boo-hooing suddenly and looked around as if she'd heard something, but shook her head and started sniffling again. Irma Jean was whispering things like, "Oh, Mama, don't go away yet. I need you to stay. You got to be here next year."

It was getting to be real confusing. I couldn't figure out if I was dreaming or awake, so I decided to float around for a while and see what else I could see. This was my second time flying, and it was more fun than the first time, in the plane, because now I was in charge, and I didn't have to stay strapped into one of them uncomfortable seats.

The hallway of the hospital got real dark and stretched out like a tunnel, and as I began to float more quickly, I saw a peculiar light up ahead. It got brighter and brighter, the brightest light I'd ever seen, but it didn't hurt my eyes none. It was all pearly and shimmery, like it was changing colors, and I wanted to get closer and closer to that pretty sight. There was a crowd of people standing in the light and watching, like they was waiting for me. Right about then, it began to dawn on me what was happening, and I wasn't sure I liked it. I felt at peace, and wasn't feeling no pain, but if these folks was expecting me to stay with them I was ready to argue my way out of the situation. I had lots of unfinished business back home. I was surprised to see there weren't no Pearly Gates! In fact, there weren't no gates at all, and no St. Peter or any other gatekeeper taking names or numbers from anybody. There were shining people smiling and calling to me, and all around them some really bright friendly things made out of light. It was too much to take in, but I figured it was a good sign that the folks was all happy. If they were mean and burning up, it would have meant I was in the wrong place.

I took a good look at some of the faces and suddenly stopped moving toward them. This wasn't at all the lineup I expected. Harriet Hanks, the cheating bingo player who nearly got me arrested, stood there bold as brass! Phil Boggs floated by, grinning and waving at me. I couldn't believe that varmint, who let the out-of-town waste trucks bring poisonous trash to Rock Bottom's landfill, made it into Heaven. Old Shadrach Egan was there, and he had lost that crazy, wild look in his eyes; in fact, he was downright pleasant.

I heard a familiar voice calling, "Emma! Emma!"

"Abner, is that you? You old cuss, where the heck are you?"

"Right in front of you, sweet boobs. I just look younger now than I did last time you saw me."

Abner was right. He looked like the dashing young fella who took me down the aisle a lifetime ago. If I hadn't been so happy to see him, I would've cried. "You devil, you!" I said, "well, I didn't mean a real devil...you know. Thought maybe you had to pay for those times you deceived me and went to see those gals dance without clothes on!"

"Emma, there's a whole lot you don't understand yet about people, and forgiveness, and mistakes that get overlooked when you really regret that you did 'em."

"You're right, young fella (here I laughed), I'm not ready for this yet. I can't see myself spending eternity shoulder to shoulder with the likes of Harriet Hanks and Phil Boggs. I'll come back, I promise, and when I do, I expect to find you waiting for me, and not with no nudie dancer, either."

"I'll be here waiting," Abner said softly, "you can count on that."

I turned to float back the way I had come, and Abner's voice called out, "Abner's Repose at Sun Up, Emma! Abner's Repose at Sun Up!" I didn't know what the hell he…I mean what in thunder he was talking about, so I kept on my way. The very bright light-things that I saw with the folks in Heaven was escorting me back through the tunnel; guess they was making sure I got all the way home.

A whole flood of thoughts pushed their way into my head, thoughts about the hard life Miz Hanks had had, how nobody ever made friends with her, but she did things in secret to make them happy. It seems she was trying to win the Bingo money that time we had the fight because she wanted to buy Christmas surprises for poor kiddies in Rock Bottom. She seemed to be saying to me, "I did it the wrong way, but I meant well." I seemed to hear the story of Phil Boggs being sicker than people knew; his head and temper weren't right, but he wasn't entirely to blame. I had a lot to think about, and was still confused, but I felt right peaceful and kind toward everybody, and decided I was going to look at folks differently from now on. As I passed Irma Jean still crying in the hallway, I stroked her hair and she looked around.

As soon as I floated back into my body, the doctors and nurses was all excited. I looked around and checked them out. The flirty nurse was standing next to me, and I said, "Well, Missy, you'd better get yourself a different fella; this one here's married." I was looking at the wedding band on his finger. The gal and the doctor looked all flustered and turned red, while an older nurse frowned at them. "But don't worry," I whispered, "you might make it to the Pearly Light just like I did."

Irma Jean come running into the room when the hospital folks told her I was back from the beyond, and in spite of me not being the hugging type, I held her real close for the first time in many years. "Honey, do you know anything about Abner's Repose at Sun Up?" Irma Jean looked puzzled and shook her head. "By the way, missy, I plan on dancing at your wedding next year. Ain't nothing going to keep me away. You finished making your plans?"

Irma Jean said, "All in good time, Mama. I want to hear about what happened to you today. First, though, look who's here." My three boys shoved each other out of the way and come to my bedside.

"Radcliffe! Emory! Duke! You come here to be with your Maw?"

"We came as soon as Irma Jean got hold of us," said Emory. "You gave us a scare, Maw. Don't try to do that heavy work no more; let us handle it."

Duke said, "The Sheriff let me out early so's I could come to the hospital and be with you. He said he was doing it as a favor to you, even though he thought you'd be better off if he didn't. Wonder what he meant by that?"

"I heard you ask Irma Jean about Sun Up, Maw," said Radcliffe, "and I know what it is: a new horse racing track in River County. You get well so's you and me can go there together. It sure sounds like you got a hot tip!"

Going against my old habits, I didn't call my boys worthless buzzards. I just hugged and kissed all of them, and that caused them to start bawling. I'm glad I come back to be with Irma Jean and the other Frick brides on their big day next year. I made up my mind to get religion so's I'd be ready the next time I had to float down that tunnel. I also decided to go with Radcliffe to Sun Up track and see if the tip Abner gave me was real.

So, this is why I agreed to write down this here testament to my trip to the afterlife, and the lessons that can be learned there if you live through it. I had to promise the nice doctor that I would try my best to give up cigarettes; I didn't want no more spells like what I had. I found out that, as mean as some folks might appear, sometimes there is a sorrow or a burden that makes them do or say things they wouldn't if they was in their right minds. I decided right then and there to change the way I judged other people, and no matter how family disappoints you, they're the most important thing in your life.

# 16

## GRANNY GETS RELIGION

*by*

*Duke Frick*

My Maw had a heart attack and a "near-death experience". She said it was more than "near" – she went all the way down a tunnel toward the Pearly Light, where she saw Pa and lots of other folks who had all passed on. When Maw come back from the Beyond she fretted about not being ready to meet her Maker yet. She said the next time she heads toward the light, she wants to be ready to give a good account of her life. I don't think she has much to worry about; she ain't even been in jail overnight, yet.

I been thinking, if I showed up one day, the folks in Heaven would have a real problem with the likes of me. Of course, most of my trouble just comes from me being in the wrong place at the wrong time. For instance, I just happened to borrow that red Mustang when the owner came out of his house all of a sudden. Another time, I was supposed to meet a buyer for some goods I had for sale, and we picked the wrong street corner for the exchange; how were we to know the Deputy Sheriff had that corner in his sights? So, you can see that I've run into a string of bad luck, unlike Maw. She has been real lucky.

Maw was determined to make things right before her next trip to Heaven, so I told her I knew somebody who could help her. My business partner, Skeeter, knew a preacher that operated in River County. He gave Revivals, and by all accounts was a hit with the ladies. He worked folks up into a lather when he shouted fire and brimstone at them, and everybody went home saved. I told Maw about him.

"Maw, how would you like to get religion?" I asked.

"Heavens, Duke, I sure do need some of that to get me ready for that Pearly Light I saw when I nearly died. Where do I go to get some?"

"In River County. There's going to be an old-time Revival next week in the camp by Mud Creek. I'm going to get some religion, too, just in case."

So it was settled; come Tuesday we hitched a ride with Skeeter because Maw don't drive and there was still a few problems with my driver's license, one of them coincidences I seem to have all the time. Skeeter, though, is successful. He borrowed some duct tape from Maw for repairs to the outside of his '81 station wagon, and we set off for the Revival.

"Miz Frick, you're gonna love Reverend Bank. He's got the gift, for sure," said Skeeter, as we chugged down Route 534 to Mud Creek Camp. "He's living proof that the righteous will reap what they sow."

"How long does it take to get saved, Sonny? I got a heap of unfinished business I got to take care of before I go back to Heaven, and I don't want to use up all my time on Revivals."

"It all depends, Miz Frick, on how saved you want to get. You can do it all in one night, or take almost a week, it don't matter to

Mr. Bank. If the demons are real stubborn, it may take longer than usual."

Two hours and a tire change later, we pulled up to the tent where people was already pouring in to get saved. Old folks, and families with kids, some sad men and women alone, and sick people on crutches was all turning out. There was strings of lights on the trees, and it looked like Christmas. Some singers in the tent was warming up, and everybody was getting excited. Maw was itching to be part of it all, and she popped out of the car almost before it died.

We got caught up in the crowd and sort of moved along with it like we was logs on a flooding river. Pretty gals in blue robes was bouncing around handing out song sheets. Somebody was a-yelling, "Come on in, brothers! Right down here, sister! Set yourselves down in the front where the Spirit can reach out and touch you!" I wasn't keen on anyone reaching out and touching me in public, although some of the pretty gals was welcome to try later on when things had quieted down. A blue spotlight was shining onto the stage, and a slick-looking fella was running around bossing people; I think he was just nervous because the Revival was about to start, and he wanted everything just right for the preacher to make his entrance. We set ourselves down in the second row so's we could get religion close up. When the slick fella held his arms up for attention, the choirs stopped rehearsing, everybody took a seat, and you could hear a pin drop.

"Brothers and sisters! This is the day! This is the day of your deliverance from the fire!" At the word "fire" I quick looked around to see where the nearest exits were, but that wasn't the kind of fire he was talking about. "There is one who can help you, one who can lead you to the light! Here he comes! Make way for the Lord's own messenger and modern-day prophet, the Reverend Monty Bank!" Just then the blue light dimmed and a blinding white spotlight came on. Another fella jumped onto the stage. He was dressed in a shiny gold suit and white patent shoes with gold shoestrings, and his slicked-back blonde hair looked like a halo. My jaw fell open because I had never seen anyone dressed like that. Skeeter was hooting and raising his arms. The slick fella yelled again,

"…and welcome our own angel, Mrs. Bank, y'all!" Out came a busty blonde lady with lots of sparkly makeup on. She was dressed in a blue fluffy dress and was shaking a tambourine. Near as I could tell, she was a cheerleader, because when she shook the tambourine and signaled to the crowd, everybody clapped and shouted.

Maw busted out laughing and pointed to the preacher's shoes. "He's wearing high heels!" she cried out. "That phony rascal's trying to look taller than he is! I'll bet his hair is bleached, too."

I didn't feel right laughing at a man of God, but he sure was a sight. At first I kind of thought he might be funny, if you know what I mean, so it wasn't right to laugh at him.

"Look at them rings!" Maw whispered. "They must be worth a fortune."

Maw was right; he wore so many flashy rings that he couldn't bend his fingers, but just held them straight out like he was always reaching to touch somebody. Kind of reminded me of a vampire in one of them scary movies.

"I could swear I've seen this preacher fella before," Maw said, "but I can't seem to recollect where. I'll remember before we leave here tonight."

He looked up toward Heaven and spread his arms way out, and tears was rolling down his cheeks.

I looked up where he was staring, and all I saw was the spotlight, so I figured his eyes was teary because the light was too strong. Then the show began.

"Brothers and sisters! Do you see it? Do you FEEL it? We are saved! If we repent and do the Lord's work, we will sing with the Heavenly choir forever!" With that, the folks in blue robes busted out with a song, *Singing and Swinging with the Lord.*

Reverend Bank called out over the noise, "Do you know what the Lord's work is, my friends? Do you know what you are called to do?"

Some worked-up lady in the audience screamed, "Tell us, brother! Tell us what to do for the Lord!"

"I'm glad you asked that question, Sister Jackson. The Lord needs us to be His hands in the world. Since you folks have to get out there and work all day, that leaves His servant – me – to spread

His Gospel. I can't spread it with an empty wallet, my friends! Could any of you travel the length and breadth of this great state without the monetary means to make it all possible? No! I'm going to ask my assistant, Frank Lee Dummer, to pass a basket around so that you can have the privilege of participating in the Lord's work. Let's hear the crinkle of paper, brothers and sisters! The clink of coins don't get you much participation in the spread of the Gospel nowadays."

"Hold on just a minute, Sonny!" It was Maw, standing up, calling and shaking her finger at the preacher. "Come here and take my hand."

Reverend Monty Bank came to the edge of the stage and bent down to take Maw's hand in his own. "Here's a believer who wants to be saved," he yelled to the folks that was dipping their hands into their pockets and putting crumpled dollar bills into the basket. "How much are you going to give the Lord, sister?" he asked. He sure didn't know Maw very well.

"Here's your answer, Reverend," Maw said, loud enough for the worshippers to hear. "Look at all them fancy rings. I bet if you sold even one of them you could do the Lord's work to your heart's content for a few months." He tried to pull his hands away from Maw's, but she held on and turned the rings over in her fingers. "My, look at that there wedding ring! Ain't that a beauty? I hope the one you gave your wife is as pretty as yours."

You could tell that the preacher was getting riled at Maw. He whispered at her, "What the hell are you doing, woman? Let go of my hands."

Maw lowered her voice. "I been setting here wondering where I'd seen you before, Reverend, and it just dawned on me. Been shopping at the TallMart lately? If I were you I'd let these folks get saved for free, and sell a couple of rings to pay my way."

"You're crazy, lady," Mr. Bank hissed, "and if you don't let go I'll get Frank Lee to escort you out of here."

In a voice loud enough to be heard back in Cornrow County, Maw said, "If I'm not mistaken, didn't the Lord send His disciples out two by two to do His work, and He told them not even to take cloaks or money bags? And He didn't even have a place to lay His head? I may not be real smart about the Good Book, but that's what I remember from Sunday school."

The rustling of paper money got real quiet, and folks stared, first at Maw and then at the preacher, who smiled kind of nervous-like. "You are right, Ma'am, absolutely right, but times has changed. How many of the disciples would have had to thumb a ride across the state to spread the Word?"

A voice called out, real loud, "You don't thumb a ride, either, Preacher! You got a brand new Escalade parked out front!"

The audience busted out laughing, and the Reverend got mad as a hornet. He was a foxy one, though, and knew how to turn a crowd.

"Tonight, my friends, we will forego the collection. It seems the Lord has spoken through His *lowly* ones. We will hear His message tonight, and tomorrow the basket will be passed again, for those whose souls have been moved to hear the Word and respond to it." With that, he gave Maw a sharp look that warned her she better watch out or she wouldn't be saved.

The choir broke out in another song, *There's Gold in the Streets of Zion*, and the preacher's wife shook her tambourine and pranced around on the stage. When the commotion settled down, the Reverend talked about how great it was going to be in Heaven. He said, "You will find a land of peace and beauty, with cute little angels on fluffy clouds and big old golden gates that open to let the righteous in and keep the varmints out."

Maw said to Skeeter and me, "It weren't like that at all; there weren't no clouds or gates, and angels is hard to describe, but cute isn't the word I'd use."

I think Mr. Bank heard her because he shot her another look that wasn't too friendly.

"Times is hard, my friends, and people is losing their jobs and homes; the one thing that will console you is your good old time religion, which never lets you down. The Spirit is inviting you to come up on the stage with me and give witness to the healing power of the faith I have preached to you. Admit to your sins before all the congregation, and you will be saved."

Skeeter shouted, "Amen!"

He shouted amen to most everything the preacher said, but I kept my comments to myself. I wasn't as taken with him as Skeeter was, but didn't want to get on his wrong side by saying contrary things.

Some folks in the audience got carried away and stood up to join the preacher on the stage and share how their terrible sins was forgiven. They meant well, but I had my own thoughts about owning up to past mistakes in public; you never knew when that could be used against you in a court of law. Skeeter stood up with them and thanked the Lord for freeing him from his addiction to tobacco. That was news to me, since I seen him smoking all the way to the Revival from Cornrow County. Maybe I was misjudging him, though; the healing must have happened suddenly just as we come into the tent.

"Ain't you coming onto the stage to witness, Miz Frick?" Skeeter asked Maw. He seemed to be getting real nervous.

"Not when I ain't done nothing to be forgiven for," she said.

The choirs started singing *My Sins is Wiped Away*.

"What about you, Duke?" Skeeter was a persistent cuss, I'll give him that. Somehow, I never figured him to be so religious, so I began to suspect he had an angle. What he said next sort of proved that in my mind. "Monty don't like it when folks don't come clean at his revivals." He grabbed me by the sleeve and started tugging at me. "And..and.. I don't get paid."

Maw heard that, and her head whipped around. "What's he paying you for, Sonny? Are you a shill for the Lord?" Her voice was loud enough that folks was gathering round to hear what she had to say. She had Skeeter by his ear, and was twisting it good; she had such a grip that he couldn't pull away to go up on the stage.

"Ow, Miz Frick! Let go! It wasn't my fault, I needed the money to get my car fixed up. He said they was all bad folks anyway, and had to pay for what they done. He found out what their secret sins were when they got all full of the Spirit, then he'd get to them later and charge them a fee to get forgiven or he'd let their families and bosses know what they'd been up to."

"Blackmail!" snapped Maw, "that dirty skunk. You hear that, folks?"

You could hear the crowd gasp and cry out; they was steamed at the preacher, and started moving his way.

"Any of you has one of them cell phones, call the River County Sheriff, and some of you big fellas pin down that varmint and keep him until the law gets here!"

All hell broke loose in the tent then, with folks pointing at the Reverend and screaming real un-Christian names at him. Some of them chased him around the stage, ripping off his gold jacket and white shoes. His blonde hair was not only messed up, it came off! He grabbed his mostly bald head and whimpered. The mad folks hogtied him with his gold shoelaces, then sat on him until the Sheriff arrived.

To Skeeter and me Maw said, "I knew I had seen this fella somewhere before. He came into the TallMart and bought two diamond brooches, one for his wife and one for the other woman. His wife got wind of it and divorced the flimflamming scallywag, and I'm betting that this here bleached floozy, Mrs. Bank, was the other woman then."

The lady in question ran crying from the stage, and I hurried to her side to give her some sympathy. Bleached or not, she sure looked pretty to me, and she seemed to appreciate some kind attention.

The Reverend Monty Bank was hauled away by the local sheriff, but his slick helper, Frank Lee Dummer, had skedaddled to unknown parts.

Skeeter took Maw's advice, "Never answer any unasked questions," and didn't volunteer any information to the sheriff. We just slipped quietly out to his station wagon and got it started after only three tries. Maw was fit to be tied all the way home; she was on Skeeter's case about his part in Reverend Bank's scam. "You little scamp! Ain't no excuse for what you done. Your Mama and Paw will be sad to find out what you done to their family name."

Skeeter was more hangdog than I ever seen him; I almost felt sorry for the poor sap. "I know, Miz Frick, I can't never make it up to them. Think you can hold off on telling them? I ain't never going to get mixed up in that kind of thing, ever again." He added, turning on his charm, "I'll do anything you want, Miz Frick – chores, errands, whatever."

Maw just looked grim and went, "Hmmph."

Maw said she didn't feel any holier than she had before the Revival, but was happy to have helped the folks who had been conned by that fake preacher. Doing a good deed, she said, was what religion was about anyway, so maybe she was saved after all.

I somehow don't think that I got religion at that Revival, so maybe I'm not saved. What I did get was the phone number of the preacher's wife, Bambi. The poor lady needs some consoling, and she has a cousin for Skeeter to console, too. Maw doesn't need to know about that, especially while she's so riled up.

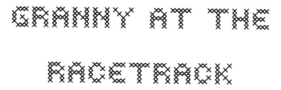

# 17

## GRANNY AT THE RACETRACK

*by*

*Radcliffe Frick*

W hen Maw came back from the Beyond, she told us how Pa had spoke to her in Heaven about Abner's Repose at Sun-Up. We kind of thought she had been dreaming while she was laying on that emergency room table. Still, it seemed odd that Pa had said Sun-Up when Maw had no idea what that was. I sure did. A really strange thing happened. When the new Sun-Up Racetrack opened in River County, I studied up on what horses would be running in the opening days. Sure enough, a 5-year-old bay named Abner's Repose was going to run in the ninth race next Saturday. I told Maw about the horse, and asked her if she wanted to go to the track with me and my girlfriend, Charlene.

"I sure do, Radcliffe. Abner wanted me to go there, so he must've had something special in mind."

I had a good feeling about our luck that day, and took a big wad of cash with me. Charlene wasn't feeling too well, but she was game to come along. Maw was getting used to the idea of us dating, and got along better with Charlene than I ever thought she would. Sometimes they acted like old friends, and talked about stuff in whispers, like I wasn't supposed to hear.

Maw was looking forward to an adventure. "I ain't never been to a racetrack before, but always did like to watch horses. Nothing prettier than a horse when it's running. My Grandpa raised horses, and my Paw knew all about taking care of them. I used to ride them around the farm. How about you, Charlene? You ever been to a track?"

"I been to lots of tracks, Miz Frick; I used to date a jockey, and he gave me tips. None of them ever paid off."

As the racetrack came into sight, Maw got real excited and couldn't wait for us to park so's we could get a good spot along the rail. I was glad we got there in time for the first two races, the Daily Double. I couldn't wait to pick the winners in both races and win a fortune. We got general admission tickets and programs. I bought me some tout sheets, but Maw said she didn't see any point.

"The fella who writes for the official program should know as well as anybody what horses are going to win," she said, "and we can guess same as he can."

There was already a big crowd when we got there, but Maw found a way to wiggle through to the rail, and dragged us along with her. Once Maw staked out a spot anywhere, no one was going to take it from her. We set up two lawn chairs for the ladies. Maw had all the necessary things for a day at the track in her tote bag: binoculars, bottles of water, pencils, and snacks. It was clear Maw was taking track day seriously. I studied the program and tout sheets, and made my picks for the Daily Double: Hard Core in the first race, and Shar-Lean in the second.

Maw said, "Radcliffe, take me to the paddocks where the horses are held before they get saddled up. I want to take a close-up look at the ones we're going to bet on."

Not wanting to leave Charlene, I complained, "Aw, Maw, there ain't no reason to go there. Only horse experts can tell what's wrong with a horse – if anything is – or which ones are going to run faster."

"All the same, I have a mind to go. Charlene will hold our spot, won't you?"

Charlene was a good sport, like always. We hadn't broken the news to Maw yet that Charlene was pregnant. That battle could wait until we were on our way home.

We went to the paddocks, and Maw was in her glory, scooting from one horse to the next.

"I like the way horses smell, Radcliffe; I always think of Grandpa when I smell manure. These animals got an instinct for people, and know when a body's sincere."

We found Hard Core, a moth-eaten wreck of a brown horse.

"You sure you want to bet on this here Hard Core? He's got only one eye, Radcliffe! Whoever heard of a one-eyed horse winning a race? He's got a mean look out of that eye, like he's plain ornery."

"Don't know about that, Maw. Slick Pick Dick says he's a shoo-in, and Shoutin' Tout says he'll move."

"There's something wrong with a man who'll make a disabled critter like that run just to make him some money. Look at him, so scared and edgy he's all frothy, and the race ain't even started yet. There was a mean farmer down the road from my Grandpa's farm, and he used to give his animals bad medicine just so's they could work hard for him, then drop in their tracks. His horses looked like that."

"Take a look at Shar-Lean, Maw. She's my bet for the second race in the Daily Double. Don't see nothing wrong with her, do you?"

"She's a gray, Radcliffe. Grandpa used to say..."

"You don't give much credence to that superstition about grays, do you, Maw?"

"Not really, but it's hard to shake off that old saying. My cousin Ferdy swore that a gray horse didn't have the endurance that others did. He said a bay could run rings around a gray any day. Tried to prove it by having a contest to see which of the horses in the valley was fastest."

"How'd that go, Maw? Did the bay win?"

"Hard to say how it would've turned out. The gray led the pack for most of the race, but got sidetracked when they ran past the apple orchard. The bay got tripped up by a green-broke paint, and when they sorted theirselves out the only horse still running was a 15-year-old bald-faced mare, so she won. Grandpa won a bundle that day because he'd made a sentimental bet on her."

"Well, my gut is telling me to go with my picks, Maw. Hard Core runs with his feet, not his eyes, so I'm going to take a chance. And Shar-Lean is *my* sentimental bet, because of Charlene."

With that, Hard Core laid his ears back, bared his teeth and tried to bite his handler. Since the handler was on the horse's blind side, he ducked just in time and didn't get bit. Looked like it was shaping up to be an interesting race.

The gray, Shar-Lean, closed her eyes and tried to snooze.

I bought my Daily Double ticket, and we shoved our way back to the rail. When the horses come parading past us, Hard Core was fighting his rider, kicking, bucking and trying to bite the little fella. The track ponies had to press him hard between two of them just to keep him under control until he was stuffed into the starting gate.

"Take the ticket back and trade it in, Radcliffe," said Maw. "That horse is a bad one and will lose the race and your money."

"It don't work that way, Maw. Once the bet is made, there's no turning back. Sometimes they scratch a horse before the race, but only if they have to, because they'll lose money. And don't get any ideas about going to the track owner and raising Cain. You won't win that argument."

Maw pouted and fretted. Guess she didn't like the idea of there being an argument she couldn't win. The horses began to line up at the starting gate, and Hard Core threw his jockey. Some men got the critter under control and the rider climbed aboard again. Inside the gate, the horse reared up and tried to climb out. I groaned and wished the race was over. At last, the man on the loudspeaker yelled, "They're off!"

Maw and Charlene was jumping up and down, and screaming for Hard Core to pull out in front.

When the horses rounded the last turn and headed for the finish line, who should be in the lead but my horse! The poor jockey didn't have to use the whip; that nag was running like a dog food canner was chasing him. He was covered in froth, his ears was laid back, and the white of his one eye was showing. He shot past the finish line several lengths in front of the second horse, and the jockey had to haul back on the reins to get him to slow down.

"You just won a bundle, Radcliffe!" shouted Maw.

"Not yet, I ain't, Maw. My bet was on two horses, and Shar-Lean has to win the second race. She's going off at 12 to 1, and I have a hunch that I just might have a winning ticket here."

We had to wait a while for the second race, but at last the bugle blew, and the horses paraded past us on their way to the gate. It was exciting to hear the sounds of the track: harnesses jingling, horses whinnying, bettors cussing. Shar-Lean looked like she was hung over – not that I would be familiar with that condition. She plodded along with her eyes half closed, like she just wanted to nap, not run around a dusty track. If she didn't wake up, I could kiss my winnings goodbye. The horse went into the gate without any trouble, and that was a relief to me. Now, if she could just get up enough energy to run...

The announcer fella shouted, "They're off!"

We all jumped up and leaned over the rail to catch sight of the pack as they came around the far turn. The board showed number 6 – Shar-Lean – in the lead, and we went crazy. The crowd was yelling, and so was the announcer. Shar-Lean was way out in front, and running like lightning; I didn't know she had it in her. So much for the superstition about grays. As she came down the home stretch, the reason for her good showing became real clear. Somewhere along the back stretch, my horse had dumped her rider, and she was breezing for the finish line wide awake and without no jockey.

The three of us just stood quietly, all droopy and sad. I tore the ticket up into little pieces and threw them on the ground.

"Twelve to one," I said. "If her jockey was still on her, I'd have won more than $700. Don't think I'm going to place any bets on the next race or two."

We decided to get some food and take a good look at the program for later in the day. The stakes races usually had better quality horses. Charlene said, "Radcliffe, I'm going to talk to somebody I used to know. You and Miz Frick hold my spot, and I'll bring some sandwiches when I come back." Maw got out some snacks, venison jerky and pepperoni rolls, to eat while we waited for Charlene.

Maw struck up a conversation with a raggy old geezer standing next to her. Personally, I didn't think she should be talking to him, but I wasn't about to tell Maw what to do. She offered him some jerky, and he said it was the best he'd ever eaten. Turned out he had a story to tell, and Maw took it all in. He said he owned one of the horses scheduled to run later that day, and strongly suggested we should bet on it. Maw was all ears .

"I ain't going to listen to no track bum, Maw, and you shouldn't, either. If he's so well-heeled, why don't he sit up in a box where all the other owners sit?"

"But, Radcliffe," Maw began, "you can't guess what horse he owns!" Being stung by my losses and annoyed at the nerve of this old fella bending Maw's ear, I said I didn't care if he owned the Kentucky Derby winner.

"You always was a stubborn cuss, son. Alright for you; make your own mistakes. This here owner knows his horses, and I'm listening to him. We got a lot in common."

Just then, Charlene came back with chili dogs, lemonade and information. "Cliff, Honey, I just talked to Raoul, a jockey I used to know – a long time ago – in Florida. He said there's a real interesting horse coming up later, in the ninth race. Want to hear about it?"

"This the jockey fella who used to give you bad tips?" Still grumpy about my losses, I was rude to Charlene and told her what Raoul could do with his information. My attention was on the races earlier in the day. Now I had two pouty women to worry about. The best way I could get on their good side again was to win big. We just watched the horses come and go for the next three races. The fifth one was a stakes race, and you could see a real difference in the horse flesh. Them stakes horses was full of muscles and good breeding. They made my Daily Double picks look like scroungy rats. Charlene's jockey Raoul won the fifth race, but from what I could tell, he was just on board for the ride; his big colt took off like a shot and finished way out in front.

I swallowed my pride and asked Charlene, "In the ninth race, does Raoul have the horse he was telling you about?"

With a look that said, oh, so now you're coming around, Charlene said, "No, Cliff. If you had given me a chance to tell you, you'd know he's not riding in that race. He's glad, too, because he says the one that's going to win that race is a well-kept secret. He wouldn't tell me the horse's name because he'd get into trouble, just said to watch out for a small ugly horse that gets big odds."

Maw said, "I know which one's going to win: Abner's Repose. Ain't no one going to convince me otherwise. You can throw your money away on all the other horses today, but I'm saving my money for one big bet on the winner that my Abner told me about."

She sure was one stubborn woman, and I was honor-bound to show her I could make some good picks on my own. The sixth race had a Tri-Betcha, which means you can bet on three horses at once to win, place and show. With only ten horses running, I figured my chances were good. Maw wanted to go to the paddocks again, so we wandered over there. These horses was as fine as the ones in the stakes race, and it was hard to make a choice based on how they looked. I read the tout sheets and went with the favorites. Charlene's friend Raoul was riding one of them, and he had just won a big prize in the fifth race.

Maw shook her head and said, "I can't tell you how to lose your money, Radcliffe, but if it was me making bets on this here race, I'd not pick the horse Raoul is riding. He just won, and it ain't his turn now. Look for a long shot to be stuck in there with two of the favorites. That way the track makes more money."

"Maw, are you sure you've never been to the races before? I could swear you're an old hand at this."

"It ain't hard to figure things out, Radcliffe. That there horse would be my choice, if I was to bet." She pointed to a chestnut tossing its head and looking around at the people. "See how he's perking his ears and watching all that's going on? He's a smart horse, and not scared at all; he can't wait to run."

I looked up Missing Cylinder in the tout sheets, and wrote him off. "He's not much of a racehorse, Maw. He ain't won nothing in six months, and he's expected to go at 25 to one odds."

Maw shrugged. "Do what you like, son. I'm just saying he wants to run today, don't you, horsey?" Then, I swear, the critter nodded his head and whinnied at Maw!

You can guess how the race went. Two of the three winners were favorites I had bet on. Raoul's horse came in fifth; it may have been my imagination, but I thought he was hauling back on the reins instead of using the crop when they moseyed across the finish line. Missing Cylinder came in first. Maw was nice enough to avoid looking at me while I tore up my ticket, but I think she was smiling a little.

My money was running out. At times like this, desperation can drive a person to get reckless. I decided to listen to Maw and bet whatever horses she liked for the seventh race. Maw, however, was not in a mood to be helpful, and she kept her mouth shut about which horses she'd pick. I studied and sweated over the tout sheets, trying to figure out practice times; placement in earlier races; jockeys' records; whether or not they was wearing new equipment; trainers; breeding; and stables. My head was spinning, and I didn't know what to do. I had already proven that I was no good at this, and it was hurting my pride in front of Charlene. I decided to ask her advice; it couldn't hurt, and I'd do no worse than I already done today.

"Honey, you got any thoughts on the seventh race? I'm stumped, and Maw's clammed up. I was thinking maybe Eenie Meanie to win and Miney Moe to place."

"I don't know, Cliff. I'd really like to have tickets on Redredred and Fuzzy for first and second places. Would you be a sweetie and buy them for me? That chili dog made me feel kinda queasy."

I kissed Charlene and thanked her for her tips, then went to the window. At the last minute I couldn't bring myself to bet on Charlene's horses in the order she wanted. It made more sense to bet on Eenie Meanie and Miney Moe to win and place, and put show bets on her picks. They'd be lucky to come in next to last, so if they showed she'd be happy. If they did win, I'd cover up by paying her the difference out of my pocket and no one would be the wiser. I held onto them because I'd be the one to collect, since she was under the weather.

As always, the commotion from the crowd got louder as post time got nearer. When the horses paraded past us on the way to the starting gate, I had to admit that Charlene's horses was mighty impressive. Rangy and muscular, the bay gelding Redredred looked like it could take on anything, and Fuzzy was broad-chested with strong haunches. Eenie Meanie, on the other hand, was a sorry sight, swan-necked and mangy. As you might expect, the outcome was easy to predict. Redredred breezed past the finish line a neck ahead of the second horse. Fuzzy, in the red colors of Hot Stuff Stables, paid twenty-three dollars to place right behind Redredred. Miney Mo, a pretty good horse, finished third. Eenie Meanie struggled to finish tenth in an eleven-horse race. Charlene was excited, squealing that her horses had both won. "Aren't you glad I didn't chicken out and get a show ticket, Cliff?" I hoped she didn't hear my answer.

I asked Charlene how she had picked Redredred and she said, "Honey, you know red is my favorite color, and that was his name!"

"What about Fuzzy?" I asked.

"Oh, his jockey was wearing red silks, silly."

"Good thing you bet on him, then." Charlene was giggling too hard to hear the sour note in my voice. I quietly tore up my own tickets, cashed Charlene's show tickets, and added money to her winnings. Maw looked at me with a twinkle in her eyes; I swear, I don't know how that woman does it. She seemed to know what happened with Charlene's tickets. Maw always did say I was a bad liar; she could read "Guilty" written across my face.

We all sat out the eighth race, me because I was broke and fed up, Charlene because she was satisfied with her big wins, and Maw because she was still waiting for Abner's Repose. At last, it was time for the ninth race. Charlene was rooting for the horse that Raoul had tipped her off about. The old fella Maw was friendly with was excited about his nag. I wasn't going to get involved; in fact, I was thinking I wasn't never going to set foot in a racetrack again. Maw dug around in her purse and come up with a handful of large bills.

"This is it!" she yelped. "I'm putting everything on Abner's Repose, then we can go home."

"You mean to show, right, Maw?"

"Not on your life, Sonny. Every penny goes on Abner's Repose to win. Abner gave me the tip, and I believe him. That's the only reason I come here today, and I never would've known Sun Up was a racetrack if you hadn't of told me, Radcliffe. This day has been hard on Charlene, in her condition. Missy, I appreciate you being here with us today, but you'd best take it easy from now on."

I was thunderstruck. "Maw! You knew all along?"

"I ain't blind, Radcliffe. You going to be part of the family wedding in June, Charlene?"

"Miz Frick, I wouldn't miss it for the world, and I thank you for being such a good sport!" With that, Charlene hugged Maw real tight.

"I still think you're making a mistake about the bet, Maw. Maybe you heard them doctors talking about the new track while you was asleep on the emergency room bed, and just thought it was Pa…" here she shot me an angry look, "but if you really want to do this, I'll place the bet for you."

"No, you don't, Radcliffe. You stay put with Charlene. I'll take care of my bets myself."

The old fella standing next to Maw's spot on the rail said, "You should listen to your mother, son. My horse is Abner's Repose, and I can vouch that he's much better than he looks. He will win this race."

"Go on, mister," I said, reading the info on Abner's Repose in the program, "you ain't Berk Fincar of Celestial Stables."

"Oh, yes, I am, Radcliffe. I enjoy watching races from the rail, where they were meant to be watched. It gives me the opportunity to meet people like your Maw, who restore my faith in humanity.

Your Maw believed me, and she believed your Pa. Just set back and watch what happens to them that believes."

Maw come back from the betting window smiling and clutching her tickets. She said the fella who sold them to her warned her to bring an armed guard with her to pick up her winnings if Abner's Repose went off at 90 to 1, then came in first. She should also be ready to talk to the IRS fella standing around waiting for the big winners. "He said, 'That nag ain't gonna see no winners' circle in his lifetime,' and I told him, just have faith; folks ain't always what they seem, and neither is horses."

I didn't want to hang around and watch Maw's savings go down the drain, but more important, I didn't want to see her heart broken. We held our breath and looked over the horses as they walked past us. The crowd broke out laughing when the last horse, number 9, Abner's Repose, limped past. Charlene gasped, "That's the ugly little horse Raoul told me about! He said it would be the most pathetic animal on the track. Please, Cliff, take my winnings and put them on this Abner's Repose to win, will you?"

Maw said, "Hear that, boy? She said, 'To WIN!'"

Well, the horse was so peculiar it woke up some weird interest in the betting crowd. Those who put money on this nag all of a sudden brought down the odds to 50 to 1. The horses reached the starting gate without any hassles, but they had to wait for Abner's Repose to drag himself into the stall. When the starting gun went off, he broke last and stayed last through most of the race. As the pack rounded the last turn and headed into the home stretch, the tote board still showed number 9 running last. Me and Charlene was down, but Maw was calm and had that little smile on her face. As we watched, a miracle happened. That little limping nag from Celestial Stables suddenly busted out of the pack and ran like a demon! Without no effort, he passed seven horses one by one as if he was flying, and he was neck and neck with the eighth horse as they neared the finish line. It was a photo finish, and when the official ruling was given out, Abner's Repose was declared the winner!

Maw turned and hugged Berk Fincar first, which I thought was not necessary. To be nice, I congratulated him on the unbelievable win, and asked why he put a lame animal into the race.

He answered, "The track found him to be fit as a fiddle. Horses is smart. They can be trained to dance, and jump. They can even learn to limp." With a smile, he nodded to Maw and Charlene and headed for the winners' circle.

# 18

## ENGAGEMENTS

---

### *Irma Jean*

T he landfill was the best thing that ever happened to me. Before I joined Ma in her protest against the out-of-town dumping in Rock Bottom, I was a drudge on the line at the pickle factory in Panhandle County. Then, fired up by Ma's enthusiasm over her cause, I found a purpose, an interest in life, and a wonderful man to share it with.

I worked closely with Hunter Tydings and Ma during the land-fill protests, and saw him in a different light than years before. We both went to Rock Bottom High School, but Hunter was two years ahead of me. I had remembered him as popular, organizational and much too lofty to notice the likes of me. He was President of his class, Valedictorian, and Editor of the school newspaper, the Rock Bottom Scoop. I belonged to the Latin Club. Hunter dated statuesque girls with good skin and blonde curls. I had acne and mousy brown, straight hair.

After graduation Hunter went to the University to study journalism; I went to work at the Perky Pickle factory as a pickle pusher. Most of the pickles are inserted into jars by machine, but one stage of the process has to be done by hand, by one worker with gloves gently easing the last pickle down tightly between the others. I was hoping to save up enough money to go to college and earn a degree in education. I took some courses at Panhandle County Community College, got an Associates' degree, and planned to finish my education after I saved up more money. That meant working odd shifts at Perky Pickle while attending classes part-time.

One day I was studying while lounging on the lawn at the college, when the groundskeeper came by on his riding mower. He was a good-looking guy, and flirted with me like I was actually pretty and popular. Naturally, I was flattered and flirted right back. That was how Ernie Beck and I ended up married to each other, and a more poorly matched couple could not be found. The only good thing to come out of the adventure was our son, Caltech.

It always bothered me that Ernie ran a strip club in back of his commercial garden shop. It bothered me even more that he was involving my gullible brother Radcliffe, encouraging him to make illegal liquor and sell it to the club patrons. Even Emory worked for Ernie from time to time. Our dreams and our worlds were too much in conflict, so we parted ways when Caltech was just a toddler; I didn't want Cal to grow up thinking that rakes, hoes and pot were anything other than what you use in a garden. Ma was sorry for me at the breakup of our marriage, but not as devastated as she had been that we got married at all. Her dislike of Ernie was bitter and hard; it is a wonder to me that she is tolerating his role as Radcliffe's best man. I guess she just wants everything to go smoothly on our mutual important day. Each couple will have their own attendants, guest list, flowers, music and catering. This three-ring circus is Ma's idea; I wanted a quiet, private ceremony and small reception for family only, but none of us want to disappoint Ma, who has her heart set on a production that would set records in Cornrow County. We are all following the plan, and will try to get along as one big happy family this time.

Ever since Hunter hired me to be a reporter for the Rock Bottom Rambler, my life has changed. He respects me as a companion and friend, not just a "cook and bottle washer", as Ma used to say. I have taken courses at the University, and am close to earning a four-year degree in journalism. As an investigative reporter, I sniff out local problems and write exclusive exposés. Hunter and I are a good team, and we hope to build up the Rambler into a newspaper of state-wide or even regional renown.

Maybe there will still be time for a little Tydings, eventually. I don't envy Radcliffe his situation, though, with a new wife and a baby both coming so close together, and him having no prospects for a good job. He and Charlene are reaping what they sowed, for sure, and it's none of my business, but a sister hates to see her brother facing a difficult life. Charlene is on the tacky side, but at least she loves him and has turned over a new leaf.

Caltech's fiancée, Laurie, is an angel, and I look forward to having her as a daughter-in-law. She's sensible, ambitious and smart. Cal has just earned a degree in criminology, and Laurie is studying to become a nurse specializing in care of the elderly. I can foresee a bright and happy future for them. Ma is tickled at Laurie's choice of a career, and said, "Laurie can practice on me someday when I get elderly – thirty or forty years from now."

I have chosen my good friend Kate as maid of honor. She is an R.N. in Rock Bottom, and teaches classes at the college Laurie is attending. We're going to wear tasteful beige shantung dresses, with peach roses in our bouquets and hair. I went through the white bridal gown debacle once, when I married Ernie. He and his groomsmen got drunk and raised Cain, spilling punch on my gown and making passes at the bridesmaids. Pa was still around then, and he gave me away against his better judgment. This time Radcliffe will do the honors, but he'll also be doing double duty as the groom for his ceremony with Charlene.

We three brides still have to work out whose music will be featured, and what foods will be served at the reception. There is a wedding consultant in Rock Bottom who can sort all this out for us, and I'm going to hire her for the occasion. I will request that Hunter and I have our ceremony first, so as to avoid the display that Charlene and her attendants will present when they come in last. The farther removed we are from her retinue, physically and figuratively, the better.

After the chaos has subsided, Hunter and I will go on a short honeymoon on a small Caribbean island, then settle down in his beautiful house, which is almost as grand as the one belonging to the funeral director. Hunter's place is on Tenpoint Hill, with a vista of the landfill where we fell in love.

# Laurie

Cal proposed to me the day after we saved Granny from getting arrested at the Bingo game. After he proposed, we got our matching tattoos at the Ratta Tattoos Parlor. We thought there couldn't be any more permanent way of showing we belong to each other than identical tats of our initials, CB and LS, wrapped around each other in a curly-q design. Since he'll be working for law enforcement as a non-uniformed investigator, there are no regulations in Cornrow County against him getting a tat. Caltech's Granny was really mad when he went around showing folks his new body art.

"In my day, nice young men and ladies did not get theirselves painted up like wild savages! Go get them things washed off your skin right now!"

Cal was nervous, and stammered, "Uh, Granny, these ain't paint, they're tattoos, and they can't be removed."

Granny was burning up and spoiling for a fight, but saw that Caltech had inherited the Frick spunk. She gave in gracefully – for her –and grumbled, "Hmmph. Well, you're the ones to live with that insult to your bodies. Mark my words, when you're my age, you'll regret you done this."

Cal whispered in my ear, "When we're her age, we'll have a dozen more tattoos, one for each kid!"

"Sez you," I shrieked, thumping him on the arm, and we giggled for five minutes.

I want my wedding with Cal to be the most perfect affair: the most beautiful, romantic, fairytale one ever held in Rock Bottom! Like a typical man, he says he just wants to get hitched, and the heck with the party. My sister, Ginny, will be my maid of honor, and three of my best friends will be bridesmaids. I can't make up my mind about what colors to choose for the wedding party; it's a toss-up between pink or baby blue, and I've even thought about a rainbow wedding. We still have a few weeks to decide all that. Cal wants my Uncle Jimmy Purgitt to be his best man because as Sheriff he inspired Cal to go into law enforcement. Cal's three uncles will have to be in the party to please Granny and his mother. I just hope they'll behave themselves and not put crawly things in Cal's truck when they decorate it.

Mother and Dad love Cal to pieces, they like Irma Jean and Hunter OK, and think Granny is a breath of fresh air, at least from a distance. Mother said, "Cal's uncles are a disgrace, and I hope you will not let them get involved in your lives." I promised to keep them at arm's length, especially when my family is visiting. Uncles Cliff, Emory and Duke have big hearts, though, and are all giving us a really great wedding gift: detailing and a year's worth of maintenance on Caltech's old pickup and my new used Myopia. I don't have many relatives, so I kind of enjoy the antics of Cal's family. Caltech's mother Irma Jean has taken over some of the wedding arrangements so that she can have things her way. She's a nice lady, but seems to think she's better than the rest of us because her fiancé is an editor. My Dad is President of Foreclosures United Bank, but I don't rub it into people.

It doesn't matter much to me if anyone approves, anyway; Cal and I have been sweethearts since third grade, and I've never even considered having another boyfriend. He can be a little rough around the edges sometimes, but I'll work on him after we're married.

I'm studying elderly care at the college. Old folks are so sweet – most of them, anyways, and the ones that aren't have problems that make them the way they are. They're always happy for a kind word and a smiling face to brighten up their day. My professors say that's my talent and I should go for it; even if my grades are a trifle low, I'll make a good caregiver. I'll be able to get jobs easy because folks in Rock Bottom are aging and soon there won't be many young people to take care of them. A few of the boys and girls we went to school with have left town to get rich in the big cities. The rest work on their family farms, or in construction, or in their Daddy's shops.

Since Caltech's Dad is no-count, my sweetie has struck out on his own. He likes to solve mysteries, and says criminal investigation is like putting together puzzles. When he solves a case, folks feel better about matters being laid to rest. In a way, Cal and me are both just trying to make people's lives better. Law enforcement is a good field for him to be in, because there's always crimes to solve, no matter how bad the economy gets, so we'll always have an income.

Caltech and me have been saving up for the wedding, and for a place to live, so I told him not to spend any money buying me an expensive engagement ring. Turns out Granny Frick had been saving, too, and insisted that Cal give me the diamond engagement ring that her husband, Abner, had given her when they got engaged. She also had saved plenty for the wedding and a down payment on a little ranch-style house just outside town on Dustdevil Lane. We won't waste money on a honeymoon; there's so much to do to get the house livable, we're just going to take a few days off to ourselves and then get busy fixing it up.

I picked out some real pretty wallpaper, paint, and ruffled curtains, and I've been looking at carpeting. I'm trying to talk Cal into buying a beautiful chandelier for our dining room, but he is balking, and said, "Ha! We're going to be as ridiculous as those folks on Tenpoint Hill, only we'll have a Tenpoint chandelier in a Dustdevil dining room!" Cal's not as excited about the house improvements as I am, but he'll see how it will make our lives more comfortable in the long run. Someday he'll invite his buddies over to watch football on TV, and I'll serve them snacks on a silver tray, and he'll be really proud to show off his nice house that we worked hard to fix up.

When we move in I'm going to plant daffodils and tulips. Oh, yes, and irises. I think we'll carry some irises in the wedding procession because it won't matter if the dresses are pink or blue, the flowers will look nice either way.

I'm going to put up bird feeders all over the yard. I was thinking about joining the Tweeters bird watching group, but Granny said don't bother: "They don't know a grouse from a chicken, and they don't got a sense of humor, neither." My sister Ginny's friend Mavis met Granny and Uncle Duke at a bird watching outing once, but she won't talk about it, just mumbles something about Betsy.

———

## Charlene

My fiancé, Cliff Frick, is the sweetest old boy this side of River County. We met when I was dancing with the Fruit Tarts, and he was selling 'shine to the customers. Everything was fun and laid back, until Cliff's Maw interfered and made the Fruit Tarts go out of business. I sort of blackmailed Miz Frick: I'd keep quiet about her family secrets if she didn't stand in the way of Cliff and me dating.

Most everybody in Rock Bottom knows the story. We outsmarted the old gal, and started dancing as the Budz in back of the hardware store. That went along fine for a while; Cliff never held it against me that I was an exotic dancer, and we figured what Maw Frick didn't know couldn't hurt us. Not that I don't like Cliff's Maw. We actually get along real good; we understand each other, and respect each other's turf. I say she's got spunk, and she says the same about me.

Something happened that made me give up exotic dancing. I got pregnant. At first I panicked, and didn't want to tell Cliff. I thought about leaving town, but my Grandma, Maude Bellows, come to Rock Bottom and talked me out of running. There was never any question about me having the baby; it was Cliff's and I loved him, so I wanted his baby. I just wished we were married.

Hanging over us was our fear of how Maw Frick would react to Cliff's engagement to an exotic dancer.

Cliff likes to say, "The Lord will provide," and darned if that isn't just what happened. JoEllen Dyer, who runs the Beehive Beauty Salon, took a shine to my Grandma and sized up my situation. "Miz Bellows," JoEllen said, "I'm overworked since my sister Bobbie went and had her baby. I need to hire another operator, and I been thinking your granddaughter Charlene would be just the kind of gal we'd like to have here. She's friendly, bright and young. Think she'd like to give it a try? I'll train her; she has real style, and she's smart enough to catch on quick."

Grandma hesitated, then said, "Maybe you don't know about her going to have a baby; she'd have to take a break then."

"Miz Bellows, don't nothing ever escape my gaze; 'course I knew. I'll train her and let her get in some practice, then after the baby comes she can come back full time. She can even bring the baby here and put up a playpen. I offered for Bobbie to do that, but she wanted to stay home."

That's why I owe my new career to my Grandma, and to JoEllen, who give me a chance to prove myself. I love doing hair, and making the ladies of Rock Bottom look as nice as they can. Someone once said, we gals owe it to ourselves to be as pretty and as young looking as we can for as long as we can; the Lord wants that for us. Well, don't know as how I go along with that last part, but it makes me feel even better about what I do. We can now face Maw Frick with our heads held high. I don't have to cover up about the Budz any more (not that we covered up much of anything there), but can talk truthfully about the Beehive Beauty Salon.

One night, while me and Cliff were parked up near Buzzard's Beak Point – watching the moon rise, of course – he said, "Sugar, I sure would like that little baby to carry my name. What say we get married?"

"We don't need to get married for it to carry your name, Cliff, so that ain't no reason to marry me. In fact, don't bother if that's the only concern you have." I was feeling a little miffed.

"Oh, no, darlin'! I never meant it like that! I guess what I was really trying to say is I love you and want you to be a Frick! Will you marry me when Irma Jean, Hunter, Caltech and Laurie all tie the knot?"

"Sure will, you big dummy! I love you, too, and been waiting for you to pop the question before our kid is born; but, do you think it's a real good idea to be part of the big wedding? Irma Jean is snobby, and Laurie's folks are uppity, too."

"You know how Maw really wants to have the whole family together at one big wedding party. This'll be our chance to stake out our claim as part of the Frick clan. All three of us." With that he grinned at my tell-tale bulge.

"That'll be the wedding of the century, Cliff! The Rock Bottom Rambler will feature it on the Society page! Grandma will be so proud of me."

Cliff give me a big ol' red stone engagement ring. I never questioned what kind of stone it is because I didn't want to embarrass him if it ain't precious. It's precious to me because he knows I like red, and he must of gone to extra trouble and expense to find me a special red ring.

Cliff and me had to find a place to live, and get everything ready for the baby. His single-wide on his Maw's property wouldn't do. As Cliff said, "The Lord provides." It seems Shadrach "Crazy" Egan's place on Turkey Hill was available because he passed away without no kin and we got it for only the back taxes owed. We'll be close enough to Maw Frick for comfort, but not convenient enough to have her there every day. We plan to continue the swapping arrangement that Mr. Egan and Maw had: chickens and eggs for vegetables and fruits.

We picked out names. Following the Frick family tradition of naming kids after colleges, we agreed on Stanford if it's a boy, and Sarah Lawrence if it's a girl. Either way, I'm excited to become a Mom, and Miz Frick can't wait for another college to be added to the Frick list.

I been busy planning our part of the wedding. My Grandma will give me away, since she's the only family I got. My maid of honor will be JoEllen, and the girls from the Budz – Tiger Lily, Daisy, and Black-Eyed Susan - will be my three bridesmaids. Naturally, they will all wear my favorite color, red, and they'll look real dazzly with sequins and feathers just like we used to wear. The flowers will all be red roses because the Budz name I danced under was Rose. I'm having a classy maternity gown made with sparkly sequins and a feathery boa, and a floor-length veil that makes me feel like a queen.

Cliff's best man will be his business partner, Ernie Beck, and his groomsmen will be his brothers Emory and Duke, and Ernie's brother Jack, proprietor of the hardware and feed store where the Budz dance. I offered to give all the fellas hair cuts and beard trims for the big day, but they refused. They all agreed with Duke, who said, "Ain't no woman going to cut my hair. It's biblical!" Something about women stealing their strength from men. Cliff made appointments for all of them at Earl's Barber Shop, and when they come out all trimmed and shined, we didn't recognize them. They might do us proud yet.

Grandma was thinking I shouldn't be so bold as to wear white, considering my condition, but Miz Frick spoke up and said, "My Mama always said every bride deserves to be a virgin on her wedding day." Coming from Cliff's Maw, that surprised me; she lets us know in small ways that she disapproves of me "being in the family way" before getting married.

It has been a long road from those days of pole dancing in Harbor City, to exotic dancing in the back room at Ernie and Jack Beck's establishments, to a bona fide hairdressing job in the Beehive. I found me a real nice quality fella and a respectable life. Sometimes I feel like I'm dreaming, then the morning sickness kicks in, and I know it's for real.

# 19

## THE FRICK WEDDING OF THE CENTURY

*by*

*Sunny Hart*

Rock Bottom was the scene of my greatest professional challenge, the Frick family triple wedding. Sunny Hart always rises to any occasion. Born Candy Hart, I have always lived up to my given name of sweetness and congeniality. Blessed with a talent for making folks' dreams come true in the wedding consultation business, I earned the nickname "Sunny" because no matter how rotten the weather before one of my weddings, on the appointed day the sun miraculously comes out and shines on the happy couple. I had high hopes that the Frick affair would maintain my record. If anyone could pull this off, it would be Sunny Hart, the Queen of the Perfect Wedding.

Irma Jean Beck, bless her heart, approached me about coordinating her wedding to Hunter Tydings, editor of the Rock Bottom Rambler, with her son Caltech's wedding to Laurie Scott, and her brother Radcliffe's wedding to Charlene the ex-stripper. The multiple affair was the brainchild of Irma Jean's Ma, Emma Frick, known as Granny. Irma Jean preferred something small and tasteful, but she didn't want to hurt her Ma, who had her heart set on the big to-do.

Granny had to be in on the doings, seeing as how she was paying for the lot out of her savings. Planning the newspaper editor's wedding would be a plum for me professionally, with free publicity. Granny was a celebrity locally on several levels, and nationally for her foray into the world of art. There was bound to be a big spread in the Rock Bottom Rambler. Most of the townsfolk, on every level of society, were invited to the wedding-times-three. I was almost as excited as the brides and Granny. This bash would give me the chance to wear my signature clingy gold lamé sheath with gold strap four inch heels; I could picture the Rambler layouts already!

No one in the weddings, including Granny, was crazy about rubbing shoulders with Radcliffe's bride, Charlene Bellows, her grandmother Maude, and the best man, Ernie Beck, Irma Jean's ex. The makings of World War III were in place. I came up with an ingenious solution to please everyone. We would not have a triple wedding, strictly speaking. Each bride would process down the aisle separately, and go to her own designated corner of the garden with her retinue. Each wedding party would be accompanied by the music of their choice. When all three parties were in place in their own spots, their chosen clergymen would perform the ceremonies simultaneously. Reception tables would be set up far removed from each other, and seating would be separate for each guest list. At the hub of ceremonial activity would be seating for Granny Frick and guests common to two or more of the couples. This arrangement would take skillful coordination and timing, but with my experience handling almost any situation, I knew I could make it happen.

Hunter and Irma Jean hired a string orchestra to play high-brow pieces, *Pachelbel Canon* and the *Processional* from Handel's *Fireworks Suite*. Caltech and Laurie wanted popular romantic music like *I Will Always Love You* and *You Are So Beautiful To Me*. Radcliffe and Charlene booked Bucky Burke and the Bail-Jumpers to play their favorite tunes, *I Love You More Than My Exes* and *I'd Pawn My Truck For You, Baby*.

I engaged my favorite caterers, Pete's Eats, best in the Tri-County region, and we had to meet separately with the three bridal factions and Granny Frick to plan their separate menus. Irma Jean insisted on being the first bride in all matters of planning.

Irma Jean said, "Ms. Hart..."

"Just call me Sunny."

"...Sunny, I'm concerned that the day will turn into a circus! I want the ceremony and reception to be tasteful. That might be impossible, given the bride my brother Radcliffe has chosen, and his friends who will be part of the festivities. I can picture Charlene's crowd getting drunk and rambunctious, dancing to raucous music and feasting on possum stew. Hunter's parents are quality, and I really want to impress them with my elegant wedding."

"Well, Missy, listen to you!" chirped Granny. "You better come down off your high horse. Elegant, you say! Whatever happened to the down-home gal who wanted pizza at her first wedding reception? Who danced barefoot in the lawn sprinkler with her hundred dollar wedding gown on?"

"Those were different times, Ma. I've come a long way since then, and really want this wedding to be the start of a new life. Please don't let Radcliffe and Charlene ruin the day for the rest of us...and...no disrespect to your specialty venison jerky, but I'd rather not feature that on our menu. I want no hoedown music, or barbecue pits, or tacky crepe paper garlands."

With that, Irma Jean took the gum out of her mouth and stuck it under the table.

Granny agreed to the terms. "Can't say I blame you for wanting to do it right this time. Guess you deserve a fancy sendoff after what you went through with that snake Ernie Beck."

Chef Pete glowered and muttered, "Ernie is my cousin," but I'm the only one who heard him.

I told Irma Jean just to leave the arrangements to me. "Sugar, I've been in this business a while, and know how to handle difficult folks. You and Hunter will have a day to remember." I was confident I could give her the wedding she deserved.

The menu chosen was edible but ho-hum, and Chef Pete could barely contain his disdain. There was a language barrier to overcome. The chef ground his teeth when he had to explain the meaning of calamari and pate de foie gras to Granny Frick and Irma Jean.

Granny snapped, "Ain't no slimy squid or goose liver going to be served at this here to-do, no matter how stuck up the new in-laws is! I'm going to have some say, or there ain't going to be no food at all. Irma Jean, you always did like them little pizzas, and so do your friends, so we'll take some for appytizers, then everybody'll be happy."

The bride wanted a traditional cake with ivory icing dripping with delicate peach and beige flowers, and she insisted on champagne ("a real expensive brand") for toasts.

Next bride on the list was Laurie Scott. Her father, Nate "the Great" Scott, President of Foreclosures United Bank, is from one of the founding families of Rock Bottom so we wanted an appropriately classy shindig. Things had to be absolutely perfect for his little girl's wedding. Laurie and her mother were easy to please. Their tastes, according to Chef Pete, were pedestrian. "All low-calorie foods, to help me keep my figure," tittered Laurie. She insisted on the wedding cake having entwined initials – hers and Caltech's – worked into the icing to duplicate the romantic tattoo she got the day of their engagement. I thought that was really sweet, but couldn't say so in front of Pete.

Laurie was against having any alcoholic beverages at her reception, but oddly enough the icy Mrs. Scott insisted. That was surprising, coming from a lady with such a haughty air, but she was almost eager to see "some kind of booze" on the menu. They compromised by choosing a white wine: "The nice kind that comes in big jugs." To placate the pouting bride, I suggested a big bowl of pink punch for the guests who choose not to imbibe. Chef Pete groaned and rolled his eyes. Granny cackled to herself, secretly pleased at the punch suggestion, and I wondered what she was thinking.

There remained only the notorious Charlene and her grandmother, Maude Bellows, to meet with Chef Pete and me – and Granny Frick, of course. Their desires were simple: plenty of beer for the groom and his brothers, barbecued ribs and corn on the cob. Granny was tickled that Charlene wanted her venison jerky and corn dogs as "appytizers". I began to detect a little bonding taking place, and breathed a sigh of relief. At her fiancé's insistence, Charlene ordered a foil-covered papier maché model of a still as the table centerpiece. I thought Chef Pete was going to have a stroke, but he held it together. The bride requested a pregnant bride figure for the cake top, but when Pete sputtered and clenched his fists she backed down and agreed to a comical ceramic of a bride dragging her mate kicking and screaming to the altar. Everything was falling into place, and in spite of the bizarre circumstances I congratulated myself on the smoothness of the arrangements with Charlene.

Since Radcliffe would give away his sister, Irma Jean, he'd be dressed in a brown tuxedo and peach boutonniere, her choice of colors; then when her ceremony was over, he'd have to run into the house and change into a groomsman's outfit with pink cummerbund for his nephew's wedding with Laurie, then another lightning change into blue jeans and red cummerbund for his own ceremony. This was going to be tricky, and the timing would have to be perfect. I was confident, however, that Sunny Hart, Queen of the Perfect Wedding, would pull off another triumph of planning and coordination.

As often happens in wedding planning, the brides began to change details. They tried to edge out each other's plans in favor of their own.

Laurie whined, "Why does Irma Jean have to be first? My Daddy is important, and I should be the first bride down the aisle!" She couldn't decide if the flowers on the cake should be pink, blue or lavender, and tried three times to make changes, but Pete's Eats wouldn't comply after the deadline.

Irma Jean complained, "I have a problem with the veggies. Chef Pete said they were going to be served Julian style, but he had promised he would be the one to prepare everything, not somebody named Julian."

Charlene was less choosy about the details; she was just happy to be "getting hitched". Her only complaint was that she wanted to switch corners of the yard with Irma Jean so that guests wouldn't think she and Cliff were being shoved into the background. "I'm going to be a Frick same as the others, and I want everyone to know it!"

Thank heaven, Granny Frick stepped into the fray on my side. "Listen to you gals, all three of you! You hired this nice Sunny lady to take care of details, and then won't let her do her job! The next one who gives her a hard time will answer to me." With that she stamped her sneaker and gave everyone her steely glare.

Finally, the big affair was one day away, and the weather was dismal. Confident in my own legend as the bringer of bridal sunshine, I remained chipper and refused to give in to gloomy forecasts. As a precaution, however, I ordered three sets of food tents, covered processional pathways, and awnings for the ceremonies. Pete's Eats was poised and ready to deliver, and Flower Power was gearing up to work far into the night on the triple order. I took my gold dress out of the cleaners, and got my hair lightened and fluffed at the Beehive. JoEllen was booked up with relatives and friends of the brides, and the next morning would be busy with the bridal parties themselves.

True to tradition, the wedding day broke sunny and promising. The ground was wet and muddy, but the plastic walkway coverings would take care of that. By afternoon the plans were proceeding like clockwork. Everyone showed up on time: three groups of musicians, three sets of flowers, three catered meals, three of everything else.

Miz Frick was in place early with her neutral outfit: dove-gray dress with a white corsage. No amount of persuasion could make Granny give up her sneakers, however. "Ain't going to stand around all day on feet what's hurting!"

Mr. and Mrs. Scott, Laurie's parents, made an entrance a bit unsteadily, like they'd been celebrating already. Mrs. Scott was wearing an exquisite blue number that surely had come from Jeers, but her blue silk shoes were mud-soaked because she couldn't quite stay on the plastic sheeting. Mr. Scott looked dazed and perplexed, like he didn't know where he was, or why. That alarmed me; I was counting on them to give this day some class.

Irma Jean's soon-to-be in-laws, Hunter's parents, were a delightfully dowdy couple, sweet and unassuming, with ruddy cheeks and gentle smiles. I wondered what they would think of the wedding's pretensions, and decided that the bride had misjudged these nice down-to-earth folks.

Most of the important people of Cornrow County showed up. The local representatives to the State legislature were there, trolling for votes. Rock Bottom Town Councilman Wheeler Diehl came resplendent in fresh tanning job, shiny suit, shiny shoes and shiny freshly coifed hair. He made excuses for his absent wife, saying she had a bad headache; some would say her "headache" was at the wedding. Mavis Oxford, President of Tweeters, came with her binoculars, to see what she could see; Viola Haze, the famous art instructor, arrived wearing a palette of filmy conflicting colors. Moore Byers, Regional Manager for TallMart, brought his stunning wife, who in my opinion would have been more stunning if she had lightened her hair; and Berk Fincar, eccentric racehorse owner and trainer, came looking like a rumpled stable hand.

Sheriff Purgitt and Deputy Buster showed up in an official car with red lights flashing festively. When Duke Frick, Radcliffe's brother and groomsman, saw the Sheriff's car he tried to run and hide and had to be restrained by the other men in the party. The third Frick brother and groomsman, Emory, had to be retrieved from the refreshments tables several times and pointed toward the assembly area for attendants.

I relaxed and gave the signal for the festivities to begin. Irma Jean, escorted by her brother Radcliffe (who looked almost civilized in his brown tuxedo), started to process down the aisle when she stopped and shrieked in horror. The musicians had gotten their places confused, and Bucky Burke and the Bail-Jumpers were grinding out *C'mon, Baby, Let's Get Hitched!* Granny Frick and Mr. and Mrs. Tydings, the dear little down-home couple, were clapping their hands and singing along. Irma Jean, sobbing, marched over to Bucky Burke and whacked him with her peach roses bouquet. Realizing the mistake they had made, the string quartet sloshed through the mud to the Beck-Tydings site, and the Bail-Jumpers switched places with them. The string quartet looked terrified when brushing past the Bail-Jumpers; a violinist went down in the muddy grass, and wept as he wiped the muck off his instrument. When the imposing notes of Handel's *Fireworks* began, the procession resumed. Hunter Tydings, his best man and brother, Tyler, and his parents were all happy, but poor Irma Jean had tears and mascara streaking her face.

Next down the aisle was Laurie, escorted by her father, The Great Scott. As the traditional *Here Comes the Bride* rang out, Laurie propped up Mr. Scott and did her best to keep him on the plastic carpet. Laurie's strapless gown revealed her romantic tattoo. Her attendants were a confectionery vision in pink fluff. Sheriff Purgitt, as best man, wore his dress uniform. Caltech dutifully wore his pink cummerbund, but his uncles refused flat out to be seen in public wearing pink. They were all decked out in the red cummerbunds and boutonnieres to be worn in Charlene's wedding party, except for Cliff, who hadn't had time to change out of the brown outfit he wore when giving away his sister. Laurie was a trooper and ignored the little chinks in her perfectly conceived fairytale wedding, even when Cliff bolted as soon as they reached the preacher, and ran through the mud to the house to change into jeans for his own wedding. Mr. Scott fell thankfully into the nearest folding chair as soon as his walk down the aisle was over. Mrs. Scott looked straight ahead in frosty aloofness, except for a genteel hiccup.

When Bucky Burke and the Bail-Jumpers burst into their processional, already tried during Irma Jean's wedding procession, Charlene and the whole party did a line dance all the way down the strip. Maybe strip is the wrong term to apply to that troupe. Maude Bellows, Charlene's grandmother, was to give her away because she was the bride's only kin; she did the line dance enthusiastically, even provocatively, in her shimmery red beaded sheath. Feather boas swished, sequins sparkled in the sun, the very pregnant bride bounced, and everyone had a glorious time clapping and yelling Yee-Haw! Even the guests and attendants for the other wedding parties joined in the laughter, in spite of themselves. Except Irma Jean, who was still weeping, and Mrs. Scott, who pretended she was on a different planet.

The preachers all prepared to hear the recitations of vows. Irma Jean and Hunter Tydings looked the perfect couple. Now that the music snafu had been straightened out and Radcliffe had vacated, the small wedding party was as coordinated and perfect as the bride had envisioned. The Reverend, from the local Episcopal church, was ancient and kindly, albeit a bit perplexed at the huge production he had unwittingly agreed to participate in. The couples were reciting traditional versions of their promises when the chaos started!

Laurie and Caltech's preacher was an old Scott family friend, and a member of her father's country club in Panhandle County. He seemed uneasy with the unfamiliar surroundings, and the motley crew of wedding participants and guests. Sheriff Purgitt as best man stood straight and snappy in his dress uniform; I saw his eyes straying to take in Mavis Oxford the birdwatcher, and her sending blushing glances in return. Mrs. Scott kept a wary eye on her unsteady husband, to make sure he didn't pitch headlong into the potted palms. As their hired band played a sappy version of *Stand By Me*, the bride and groom held hands and gazed at each other with studied concentration. Just as they started to pledge undying love, with references to bluebirds and blossoms, a commotion broke out!

There was a stir in Charlene's and Radcliffe's corner. In a flurry of panic, the sequined and feathered bridesmaids fluttered around the bride, who was doubled over and clutching her prominent belly. Radcliffe was running in circles, yelling for a doctor. "The baby's coming! Somebody call the Rescue Squad! How you doing, sugar? Just hang in there, don't do anything yet!"

My stomach did flip-flops, and I nearly fainted. How could this happen to me? My reputation as Queen of the Perfect Wedding was going to be smirched by this...catastrophe! I am ashamed to admit I screamed at Charlene, "Hold it right there! You're ruining everything; hold it in until the weddings are over!" I was thinking only of myself, with no regard for the mother-to-be or her little one.

With my usual verve, however, I pulled myself together and circulated among the guests. My voice may have sounded trembly, but I put on the show of my career. "Howdy, Miz Oxford, Miz Haze. How y'all doing? The weather did hold up nicely, don't you think? Did you ever before hear such a rendition of *Stand By Me*?" And so it went.

Irma Jean ran unceremoniously through the mud in her beige satin shoes, orange roses flying. "Radcliffe! My friend Kate, the maid of honor, is a nurse. She's coming to help out. Take Charlene into Ma's house and lay her down on a bed." Seems that a crisis will mend even Frick family fences.

Caltech, Deputy Buster and Sheriff Purgitt came from another direction. Caltech cried, "Uncle Jimmy is here! We're in luck."

"I done called in a Rescue Squad, Cliff." said the Sheriff. "Take care of that little lady and we'll have her to a hospital in no time!"

Charlene was wailing that things were happening fast, and they'd better hurry.

Granny Frick and Maude Bellows were elbowing each other out of the way in a contest over who was to be in charge of the childbirth. "She's my granddaughter," snapped Maude, to which Granny shot back, "And this is my house and my wedding reception. Back off, *Lottie*, and let's help my son's wife to have their child." To the Sheriff she said, "Jim Purgitt, you know that by the time old Ervil gets that ambulance way out here to Thistleburr Lane the baby's going to be reciting his ABC's. I think you and Billy better go over the birthing procedure because you're going to assist Nurse Kate." With that, she headed for the house to prepare a bed for Charlene. "Oh, all right, Maude, come on. You can help with things."

"Wait! Not yet!" called the bride. "We haven't said our vows yet! Cliff, honey, bring the Reverend over here and make this official before the baby comes."

The flustered preacher ran alongside Charlene as Cliff and his best man carried her across the muddy shortcut to Miz Frick's house. JoEllen Dyer, the matron of honor, trotted alongside and held Charlene's hand for reassurance. Bucky Burke and the Bail-Jumpers played the recessional with verve: *Gonna Be a Long Night, Darlin'*.

The preacher asked breathlessly, "Do you, Radcliffe, take this woman...."

Radcliffe yelled, "Yes! Get on with it! Get 'er done!"

The next question was directed at Charlene, who was puffing futilely as she tried to keep ahead of the contractions. "Do you, Charlene, take this...."

She moaned and said, "Uh-huh. 'Course I do-ooooohhhhh!"

The other wedding vows were disrupted. Irma Jean's maid of honor and witness, Kate the nurse, was accompanying Charlene and giving Sheriff Purgitt and Deputy Buster instructions. Cal's best man was the sheriff, now tied up with a childbirth.

Once the blushing pregnant bride was tucked away, the triple receptions commenced. Instead of each wedding party staying in the designated reception area, the guests moved from table to table, sampling all the cuisine and the music. I had all I could do to stay on top of things, and my gold strap heels sank into the mud more than once as I cut across the grass from one tent to another. It occurred to me that at least two of the couples had not yet legally pronounced their vows; we would have to take care of that later.

The horse breeding tycoon, Mr. Berk Fincar, was kind gentle-man during this time of chaos, bless his heart. He helped to orga-nize the crowd and had a talent for making folks laugh instead of frown. Everyone in each reception group remained in good spirits and mingled with guests from the other receptions, with Berk - I mean Mr. Fincar – leading the way. We had a really good time talking with each other, and I've asked him to come to dinner sometime and I'll fix him the best barbecued ribs he's ever tasted. He may not look like much, but he has a heart of gold and he puts a body at ease. I think he wouldn't mind if I didn't get all gussied up, but just relaxed in sandals and cut-offs when he comes to visit. I digress; this is not relevant to the wedding.

Laurie's father, Nate Scott, lurched toward me with a lecherous gleam in his eye. "Say, Bunny! How'd you like a little snort of this awful punch? Then maybe we can find a corner and make out." When I gave him the cold shoulder he was not discouraged, but sought out the young, curvy wife of Charlene's and Radcliffe's preacher. Her name, I found out later, was Bambi, and she had previously been married to a Revival preacher who was currently doing time for fraud and extortion. She was more receptive to Mr. Scott than I had been. Maybe she wanted to escape the attentions of Duke Frick, who was following her around like a puppy.

Whenever Granny Frick trotted outside to report on the progress of the labor, she went to the controversial pink punchbowl and added something to it from a Mason jar. I decided not to make any inquiries. The punch proved to be more popular than Irma Jean's champagne; Emory Frick was glued to that table, and even Laurie's mother, Mrs. Scott, couldn't tear herself away from it. I take full credit for suggesting the pink punch; it was amazing to see so many guests choosing the non-alcoholic drink over white wine, champagne or beer.

One of the guests produced a deck of cards, and an impromptu poker game started. Two dancing areas opened up, one for slow romantic dancing with Laurie's and Caltech's pops group, and one for livelier country fare. In the Scott wedding corner, the proper guests sat around drinking and listening to Vivaldi.

Councilman Diehl snuck off to the tractor shed hand in hand with one of Charlene's bridesmaids; they seemed to be old acquaintances. Acquaintances is an understatement for their relationship, but it's not my place to judge. I am the soul of discretion, and would never destroy the illusion of perfection at a wedding. The unlikely lovebirds emerged later looking sheepish; Mr. Diehl had red sequins and bits of feathers clinging to his shiny suit.

Moore Byers, the TallMart Regional Manager, and his wife Carol struck up a conversation with Hunter Tydings and his bride Irma Jean. They swapped tales about Granny Frick, and compared notes on running their respective businesses. Irma Jean beamed and basked in the reflection of social greatness, and I knew that her future would be one of upwardly mobile euphoria. Hunter agreed to run a piece about the new and improved TallMart automotive department, and Moore made plans to take out ads in the Rock Bottom Rambler. It was a win-win situation, and an entrepreneurial union was born.

Radcliffe came outside from time to time, looking frazzled and rumpled. He joined the poker game, but kept his attention partially glued to the house where his bride was in labor. The Rescue Squad showed up and went inside to take over, now that labor was almost over. Finally came the moment all were waiting for. Granny Frick and Maude Bellows emerged from the house together, all smiles, but shoving each other to be the first to make the announcements. "It's a girl!" said Granny, "and her name is Sarah Lawrence Frick!"

"They're going to call her 'Sally'" said Maude.

"Don't make no difference what they call her, she's officially Sarah Lawrence," retorted Miz Frick. "Don't go starting something now, you..you..Great-Grandma!" To the bands she cried, "Let's have some dancing music! I promised Laurie and Caltech I'd dance at their wedding some day, and the time has come."

The pops band played *Moon River*, and Bucky Burke stepped up to Granny. "May I have this dance, Ma'am?" It was the first time any of us had ever seen Emma Frick speechless and overcome. Her mouth gaped open and she clutched her throat like a person stricken. She recovered enough to smile coquettishly and say, "Why, certainly, young man!" It was the first time in anyone's recollection we had seen Miz Frick blush.

Radcliffe rushed inside to see his new family, and made the decision to send Charlene and Sally to the hospital to be checked out and make sure everything was okay. He seemed to have grown a bit older in the past few hours.

Berk Fincar spun me around the dance space, and for a few minutes I forgot to be Queen of anything. "I would like to show you around my horse farm," said Berk. "There's a special horse I'd like you to see. Have you ever heard of Abner's Repose?" He went on to say he would like me to coordinate an entertainment for the racing crowd, and I responded that I'd love to. Horses always used to scare me, but somehow I knew that I'd feel safe with this comfortable man showing me around the stables.

Sheriff Jim Purgitt and Mavis Oxford found a quiet corner to catch up on old times, and Mavis didn't need her binoculars. Deputy Sheriff Billy Buster, a nice young man with a serious demeanor, asked Viola Haze to dance, and they glided along dreamily while the world went by. Nate the Great Scott snored loudly from a lounge chair, while his wife stood guard over the punchbowl.

Just then I remembered something very important, and made an announcement. "Hold on, everybody! We have some unfinished business. Laurie and Caltech, Hunter and Irma Jean, bring your preachers over here and pronounce your vows! The ceremony was interrupted, and you haven't officially tied the knot yet!" Both couples then went through their paces, the Tydings couple traditionally and the Becks with flowery promises and naïve dreams.

When the Rescue Squad brought the new mother and her baby out of the house, there were oohs and aahs and congratulations flying. Then, from the stretcher Charlene tossed her bridal bouquet of red roses into the air; it landed unceremoniously in Mavis' arms and the whole party burst into applause. Later, Irma Jean's bouquet was caught by Daisy, one of Charlene's bridesmaids, and Irma Jean started crying. Laurie's bouquet of purple irises hit me on the head while I was talking to Berk.

The three receptions had merged into one, with happy chaotic abandon. All parties circulated without order or purpose, and a good time was had by all. There was a time when I would have been mortified to see my carefully planned event degenerate into a madhouse, but not now. Chef Pete was the only disgruntled person. He muttered dark words as he packed up his equipment and headed out, but on the way the guests complimented him on the food and drink, especially the pink punch and tiny pizza hors d'oeuvres; this only served to make him angrier, and I made a mental note to use another caterer next time.

None of this would have been possible without the intrepid Emma Frick. Her determination and my talent together made the social gathering of the century possible in Rock Bottom, a town that definitely has nowhere to go but up, and the future was looking bright for all of us.

Made in the USA
Lexington, KY
25 January 2012